Ready, Set, RELAX

"Ready . . . Set . . . R.E.L.A.X. is an outstanding, innovative resource for teaching relaxation skills and building self-esteem. This comprehensive, research-based program picks up where others leave off by providing specific, skill-based relaxation activities and, most importantly, a systematic process for learning to apply these skills in many settings.

The program empowers the child to take an active and productive approach towards handling the many stressors he or she may face at school, home, and in the community. It is useful and effective for work with groups as well as more individualized programs, and can be implemented easily at school or home."

Rick Clark, Psy.D.
Psychologist
St. Francis Children's Center
Milwaukee, Wisconsin

READY, SET, RELAX

A Research-Based Program
of Relaxation, Learning and
Self-Esteem for Children

by
Jeffrey S. Allen, M.Ed.
and
Roger J. Klein, Psy.D.

INNER COACHING
Watertown, Wisconsin
1996

Printed in the United States of America on acid-free paper.

Publisher's Cataloging in Publication Data
    (Prepared by Quality Books, Inc.)

Allen, Jeffrey S.
        Ready, set, relax: a research-based program of relaxation,
    learning, and self-esteem for children / by Jeffrey S. Allen
    and Roger J. Klein. — 1st ed.
        p. cm.
    Includes bibliographical references and index.
    LCCN: 93-90702
    ISBN 978-0-9636027-0-1

        1. Stress in children.   2. Relaxation.   I. Klein, Roger J.
    II. Title.

    BF723.S75A55   1996   155.4′18
                                                 QBI96–20069

Artwork by Julie Cuccia Watts and Matthew Holden.

Published by
Inner Coaching
1108 Western Avenue
Watertown, Wisconsin 53094

(920) 262-0439

ELEVENTH PRINTING

This book is dedicated
to our children
Benjamin and Rachel Allen
Bradley and Kendra Klein

Contents

Part 1
Stress, Relaxation, and the Ready, Set, R.E.L.A.X. Program

Part II
The Ready Set, R.E.L.A.X. Program Scripts

Release Scripts

Enjoy Scripts

Learn Scripts

Appreciate Scripts

X-Pand Scripts

Part III
Appendixes and References

"Thoughts in your mind have made you what you are, and thoughts in your mind will make you what you become."
—Geraldine Ponder

Preface

Ready . . . Set . . . R.E.L.A.X., unlike many current books on relaxation, is based on two years of comprehensive research. This research was conducted because of our concern about the debilitating effects of stress on children. We examined the use of music, relaxation and positive thinking on children's self-report of anxiety, depression and self-concept. Statistically significant gains in self-esteem and significant decreases in anxiety and depression were recorded for children who participated in the program. Additionally, in the second year of the study, significant increases in achievement on group test results were demonstrated.

Ready . . . Set . . . R.E.L.A.X. can be used as a preventative mental health program for an entire school population, smaller groups or on an individual basis. Classroom teachers, school and mental health counselors, nursing staffs and parents are using this program both as a preventative tool as well as an intervention strategy for high risk populations of children. By purchasing this book you have taken the first step in making a real difference for many children who need to hear positive messages and find ways to cope with an increasingly stressful world.

Whether you work with many children or one child the Ready . . . Set . . . R.E.L.A.X. program can give you the tools to build a better world.

Jeffrey S. Allen, M.Ed.
Roger J. Klein, Psy.D.

Acknowledgments

Many individuals have contributed to the success of the Ready . . . Set . . . R.E.L.A.X. program over the two years of original research, the pilot year and in the subsequent writing of this book. This list is headed by our wives **Vicki Allen**, a kindergarten teacher in the Watertown School District and **Nancy Klein**, a teacher of reading and learning disabled students in the Oconomowoc School District. Both are responsible for writing the activity suggestions at the end of the scripts, proof reading and believing in us and the worth of this project.

Special thanks to the staff, parents and students of St. Bernard's Catholic School, Watertown, Wisconsin who gave their total cooperation and spurred us on with their enthusiasm for the Ready . . . Set . . . R.E.L.A.X. program. Original illustrations were created by **Matthew Holden**, a sixth grade student at St. Bernard's School. Matthew participated in the program from the beginning and, as you will see, captured its feeling with impressive childlike artistry. The cover of this book was designed and beautifully painted in oil by **Julie Cuccia-Watts** of Watertown. Julie, the mother of three young children, was inspired by her belief in the goals of this project. Self taught, she has shared her considerable talents in many other publications.

Also making contributions were Barbara Lambert (front and back cover layout), Sue Becker, Pat Klecker, Diane Schmidt, Helen Fenske, Mary Wanke, Rev. Thomas Marr, Joyce Byrne, Susan Freeman, Cathy Egan, Karyn Zick Miller, Joanne Stout, Teresa Swiggum, Karen Kwapil, Kathryn Wickmann, Ellie Zgonc, Charles Wallman, Peter Lorenz, Francine Butzine, Tom Batiuk, Jeanne Mallach, Sharon Zastrow, Sue Witt, Dina Visuri, Kelly Melcher, Shelly Degrandt, Robin Radocay, Shirley Allen, Amber Erceg and Greg Britton.

Part I

Stress, Relaxation, and the Ready, Set, R.E.L.A.X. Program

1
Stress and Our Children

"Every time we have to chose up sides for a game, they never pick me, even last. They don't want me on the team."

9-year-old Tom

"He can't live with us anymore, my daddy, because he was mean to my mother and hitted us kids when we didn't even do anything. And I stayed at his new house and he didn't hit me and he gave me this doll."

7-year-old Michelle

"I can't never do the part with the take-away numbers. I did all the problems real fast and she put big red X's on them and said I wasn't trying. And I started crying inside but I couldn't because they would all see."

8-year-old Izzy

These student self-reports, detailed by Wertlieb, typify the stresses of middle childhood. The public's interest in stress has intensified in the past fifteen years. Books and workshops abound on how to deal effectively with stress. Employee Assistance Programs offer workshops, counseling and physical fitness programs intended to reduce the stress levels of workers. It is common to find articles about stress in daily newspapers or popular magazines.

The public is increasingly aware of stress and its effects on children.

Much of this interest may be due to the results of Freedman and Roseman's research on Type A and Type B behavior. They described the Type A person as excessively competitive, with a chronic sense of time urgency, accompanied by the feeling of always having to meet deadlines. They believed that when someone is continuously engaged in a struggle to overcome time, accumulate income, and outdo competitors on both business and social levels, negative stress is the result.

Freedman and Roseman determined that serum cholesterol was affected by the Type A pattern. According to their findings:

> We found that subjects severely afflicted with (Type A) behavior pattern exhibited every blood fat and hormone abnormality that the majority of coronary patients also showed. In other words, the same blood abnormalities that so many of our colleagues believe precede and possibly bring on coronary heart disease were already present in our Type A subjects. To us the logic is irresistible. The behavior pattern itself gives rise to the abnormalities.

These results were important in that they suggested that personality characteristics may be causal factors in organic disease. Thus, not only does pressure from the outside cause stress, but personality dynamics on the inside may also result in stress. As a result of Freedman and Roseman's research, the media became very interested in the field of stress. Currently, the interest in anxiety and stress is so great that an entire periodical, the *Journal of Human Stress*, is devoted to the environmental influences of stress on health and behavior.

Experts estimate that up to 75% of all medical disorders are directly influenced by stress. In addition to the link to the development of coronary heart disease and other life-threatening diseases, psycho-social stressors may also cause gastrointestinal problems, including peptic ulcers and ulcerative colitis, skin disorders such as eczema, headaches, hypertension and respiratory ailments such as asthma. Recent research has also identified specific effects of stress: changes in lymphocyte levels, a strong risk factor for cancer; immunoreactivity; and sodium and fluid retention that cause hypertension.

The growing suicide rate in the United States and high incidence of depression have also been correlated with stressful life events. Loss, by either a broken relationship or the death of a close friend or spouse, is cited by researchers as one of the major stressors in life. Other examples of stressful life events include change of status in one's job, illness, moving and financial problems.

Experts estimate that up to 75% of all medical disorders are directly influenced by stress.

Stress Inventory

Following is a list of stressful events as adapted from the Holmes–Rahe Life Stress Inventory (modified for children). These events are ranked in decending order starting with the most stressful events.

To take the test check any of the events that have occured in the child's life in the past twelve months. The total score measures the amount of stress the child has been subjected to in the one year period and can be used to predict his/her chance of suffering serious illness within the next two years. For example, a total score less than 150 means that the child may have only a 37 percent chance of becoming ill. A score between 150–300 increases the chance of getting sick to 51 percent. A score over 300 increases the odds of getting sick to eighty percent.

LIFE EVENT	MEAN VALUE
1. A parent has died.	100
2. Parents have divorced.	73
3. Parents have separated.	65
4. Separation from parents.	63
5. Death of a close family member.	63
6. Major personal injury or illness.	53
7. Remarriage of a parent (getting a new parent).	50
8. A parent was fired *or* you were expelled from school.	47
9. Parents got back together after separating.	45
10. Parent stops working to stay at home *or* returns to work.	45
11. Major change in health or behavior of family member.	44
12. Pregnancy of family member.	40
13. Problems in school.	39
14. Gaining a new family member (e.g., birth, adoption, grandparent moves in).	39
15. Major school change (e.g., class or teacher change, failing subjects).	39
16. Family financial state changes a great deal (much better or much worse off).	38
17. Death or serious illness of a close friend.	37
18. A new activity begins (one that takes up a lot of time and energy, e.g., dance or music lessons, sports team, computer classes after school).	36
19. Major change in the number of arguments with parents or brothers and sisters.	35
20. Feeling threatened (trouble with a bully or a gang).	31
21. Losing or being robbed of a valuable or possession.	30
22. Major changes in responsibilities at home (e.g., must help with many chores or with raising a younger child).	29
23. Brother or sister leaves home (e.g., runs away, joins army, goes away to school).	29
24. Trouble with relatives other than parents or siblings (e.g., grandparents, aunt, uncle).	29

(Continued on next page.)

We need to break the cycle of stress in our children's lives.

Stress Inventory (con't.)

LIFE EVENT	MEAN VALUE
25. Outstanding personal achievement and recognition	28
26. Major changes in living conditions (e.g., neighborhood gets much improved, fire damages part of home).	25
27. Personal habits change (e.g., style of dress, manners, people you hang out with)	24
28. Trouble with a teacher	23
29. Major change in your school schedule or conditions (e.g., new school schedule, more work demanded, using a temporary building).	20
30. Change in where you live (even in the same building).	20
31. Changing to a new school.	20
32. Major change in usual type or amount of recreation (e.g., more or less time to play).	19
33. Major change in religious activities.	19
34. Major change in school activities (e.g., clubs, movies, visiting friends).	18
35. Major change in sleep habits.	16
36. Major change in family get-togethers (many more or less).	15
37. Major change in eating habits.	15
38. Vacation.	13
39. Christmas or birthday.	12
40. Punished for doing wrong.	11

Stress and Children

Most of the attention in the field of stress research has been directed toward adults, with little attention paid to the study of stress as it affects children. Children seem to be the last segment of our population with whom society in general becomes concerned. In 1988 Humphrey examined over 3,000 items of literature pertaining to stress and estimated that only 10-12 percent were devoted to stress in childhood. In addition, the literature reveals little information concerning methods of avoiding or reducing stress in order to prevent stress related disorders.

Type A Behavior and Children

One of the first long-term studies dealing with the negative effects of stress on children was done in 1983 by Hunter and Berenson. They found that early Type A coronary-prone behavior patterns indicate some correlation between psycho-social factors and cardiovascular risk in children and adolescents. A number of other researchers have also confirmed the existence of the Type A Behavior Pattern (TABP) in children. In children, TABP is characterized by excessive competitiveness, chronic time urgency and easily-aroused hostility.

Stress and the Family

In addition to the TABP, it has long been known that children's reactions to stress in general can have a negative physiological and/or psychological impact. According to Brenner, negative stress in a child's life can range from ordinary to severe. At the *ordinary end* are events which occur for most children in our society and for which there are fairly well-defined, appropriate, coping patterns. For example, most parents are aware that older children are likely to be jealous of newborn siblings. They generally know the ways in which older children usually act out their jealousy and how they can be helped to cope with this problem.

Stressful events fall along an entire spectrum

At the midpoint of the spectrum are the stresses which might occur when children are in a one-parent family. Within recent years, both the media and schools have focused more attention on the one-parent family. This has provided avenues for children to help themselves define their problems and seek constructive solutions.

An example of stress toward the *severe end* of the spectrum is the separation of children from their parents or siblings. Not as much help is available to this group of generally lonely children. Some are well cared for, while many others are ignored when there is a separation caused by divorce, death, illness, incarceration, or foster placement.

At the severe *extreme* of the spectrum are those stressors which are so long-lasting that they require the child to make major personality changes to survive. Victims of incest, for example, have no coping guidelines prepared for them by society. The number of children suffering from stress at this end of the continuum is frightening. Salholz, in a 1982 *Newsweek* article, estimated that physical violence occurs in nearly half of all families. Recent research verifies this continued pattern of violence. In addition, reliable surveys indicate sexual abuse affecting at least one in four girls by age 18. Finally, serious alcohol and other drug problems have been identified as existing in 25%-33% of families in America.

Stress and the Modern Media

Children are fairly resilient and cope with stress through creative play, which often serves as a source of healing for them. However, even this vehicle of coping is being undermined by the countless hours of television watching. According to one study the average 18 year old has spent nearly 16,000 hours in front of the television, while only 13,000 hours are spent in the classroom. The content of television programs is also troubling. One study indicated stated that one third of all TV characters portrayed on the screen supported themselves by fighting crime or by committing it. He states that the firing of guns is so common that a typical night in front of the TV set can be compared to an evening spent in a shooting gallery. In TV's world, murders are more common, and crime occurs about ten times more often, than in the real world.

And what has television taught our children in relation to dealing with stress? It emphasizes the "thirty minute miracle" in which all problems are resolved within the space of thirty minutes or one hour, depending on the length of the show. Commercials sell products to relieve stress-related symptoms. This results in virtually all Americans reaching for an aspirin or equivalent as the primary or only solution when they have a headache. No one has taught them relaxation techniques, listening to soothing music, or taking a walk as ways to alleviate a headache.

Video-cassette recorders, computers and videogames have brought social taboos and replaced creative play in many children's lives. Adult films with brutality, violence, sexual explicitness, horror and more, "entertain" a growing number of elementary school children. Newspaper headlines and magazines in the home also portray the world as a scary place. Murders, kidnapping, assassinations and natural disasters, even make adults wonder if it is safe to leave home! Countless numbers of children are exposed to such events through headlines, pictures,

The average 18-year-old has spent nearly 16,000 hours in front of the television, while only 13,000 hours are spent in the classroom.

and news broadcasts, yet have no adult with whom to talk or discuss this overwhelming volume of bad news.

Stress and Expectations

Another source of negative stress on children was pointed out by Elkind in his book, *The Hurried Child*. He believes that many parents place an inordinate amount of pressure on their young children by expecting too much from them. Elkind feels that parents strive to have their children be the best, when developmentally they are often incapable of meeting their parents' standards. Society in general seems to be following this trend by lowering the age for formal schooling. Now that kindergarten for five-year-olds has become virtually universal in the nation's schools, demand is rising to make formal instruction available to all four-year-olds. Pre-kindergarten programs with heavy educational components for children as young as 3 years old are also on the increase. Much of this has resulted from the need for alternative care due to the overwhelming majority of parents who work outside the home. As children advance in school, pressures increase. Increase in amount and difficulty of homework, competition for grades, fear of not being promoted and peer-pressure are a few of the many situations in the school setting that can add to a child's level of stress.

Children feel pressure at an early age from well-intentioned adults.

Stress and Society

It has been the authors' observation that the number and severity of childhood stressors has increased dramatically in the last ten years. The Joint Commission on the Mental Health of Children as early as 1969 estimated that almost one third of children showed school maladjustment (behavioral and emotional difficulties). Brenner reports that people who work with children relate an uneasy sense that children today have fewer sources of adult support, affirmation, and love than in the recent past. In fact, the number of children living in single-parent homes has more than doubled since 1960. It has been estimated that soon half of all children will live in single-parent homes. Also, in the last thirty years, there has been a four-fold increase in the number of youngsters living with mothers who have never been married. Other researchers have concluded that within the last fifteen years children have experienced a great deal of stress, that they have many fears and anxieties, that they worry more than adults might suspect and that they wish their lives could be emotionally rich.

The traditional therapy-centered approach is an inadequate model to deal with the large number of children affected by negative stress.

Need for Intervention

The traditional therapy-centered approach is an inadequate model to deal with the large numbers of children suffering from stress-related problems. Even if there were adequate numbers of trained therapists, only the most severe cases are generally offered a therapeutic intervention. Of those cases, many parents refuse or are hesitant to become involved in the mental health-care system. Managed care adds to the frustration of offering traditional mental health services. The high numbers of children under stress, coupled with the severity of the problems the authors have witnessed among children, were convincing arguments for a redirection of their energy into a primary prevention program.

Ready, Set, R.E.L.A.X. differs from most stress management programs because of its solid research base.

The intervention program we developed can be used with individual students, a classroom, or on a school wide basis. The program is called *Ready, Set, R.E.L.A.X.* (Release, Enjoy, Learn, Appreciate, Expand) and was designed to help elementary-age children develop specific strategies to cope with stress. The school is a natural delivery system for a primary prevention program because the potential to reach virtually every child is available. *Ready, Set, R.E.L.A.X.* is also easily adaptable for use at home, in a counselor's office or in a medical setting.

Ready, Set, R.E.L.A.X. differs from most stress management programs because of its solid research base. The program was developed over a period of three years and includes an in-service program for parents, teachers and students, the delivery of relaxation and success imagery scripts and the playing of relaxation-inducing music. Additionally, during the first two years of development, pre- and post-testing of students' self-reports of anxiety, self-concept, and feelings of depression were statistically analyzed (see Chapter 5 for results). Questionnaires completed by the students were also used to obtain feedback. (See Appendix E.)

2
Effects of Stress

In order to understand the current view of stress, it is important to review the historical components of this concept. The following review of stress is an outline of the work of Walter Cannon, Harold Wolff and Hans Selye. Of these three, Hans Selye is considered to be the "father" of stress-related research. Walter Cannon used the term "stress" in a physiological sense. The fight-or-flight response was first described by Cannon in 1914. He described it "as an emergency reaction that prepares an animal for running or fighting. Changes within the body include an increase in all of the following: blood pressure, heart rate, respiration, body metabolism and blood flow to the muscles of the arms and legs."

Similarly, most investigators who study animals in an attempt to identify behavioral/physiological interactions also equate stress with the stimulus. Many scientists who study human behavior also conceive of stress as a stimulus. These investigators believe that the stimulus itself creates stress without any intervening variables. Thus, a loud noise alone, acting as the stimulus, would be expected to create stress for the organism.

However, there are several investigators who define stress as an interaction between the environment and the individual. Harold Wolff in 1953 defined stress as "the interaction between the external environment and the organism with the past experiences of the organism as a major factor." Therefore, using the example of a loud noise, Wolff would say that the organism's experiences with loud noises would dictate whether it was stressful. If in past experiences loud noises were associated with some type of pleasurable event, they might not elicit a stress response. More recently, Williams has proposed an interactive model of stress that includes innate or acquired characteristics of the organism, which interact with the environment to produce "qualitatively different

Stress creates many physiological changes.

patterns of response extending across many response systems. . . ." This particular model emphasizes the uniqueness of each organism. It takes into account the importance not only of past experiences but, also, of inherent constitutional factors within the organism.

One of the most influential scientists in the field of stress is Hans Selye. In his 1956 book, *The Stress of Life*, Selye recounts how the work leading to his stress concepts was initiated originally in a search to discover a new sex hormone. In these experiments, Selye found that injections of crude ovarian extracts into rats produced a "triad" of changes: 1) adrenal cortical enlargement, 2) atrophy of the thymus and other lymphatic structures and 3) deep, bleeding ulcers of the stomach and duodenal lining. Since no ovarian hormone known at the time produced such a triad of physical changes, he concluded that the changes might have been simply the result of the "toxicity" of his relatively impure extracts. In pursuing the next question of how many other agents might be able to produce this same response triad, Seyle obtained similar results with a variety of additional stimuli such as adrenaline, insulin, cold, heat, X-rays, mechanical trauma, hemorrhage, pain, forced muscular exercise and nervous stimuli. He concluded that this triad, or syndrome, represented a non-specific response to virtually all noxious stimuli, and suggested that it be called the "general adaptation syndrome."

The human body is effected by stress in predictable ways.

This syndrome consists of three stages: an "alarm" reaction, the "resistance" stage and the "exhaustion" stage. In the first stage the body reacts to the stressor and causes the hypothalamus to produce a biochemical "messenger" that causes the pituitary gland to secrete adrenocorticotrophic hormone (ACTH) into the blood. This hormone then causes the secretion of adrenalin and other corticoids. This secretion causes shrinkage of the thymus and a concomitant influence on heart rate, blood pressure, respiration rate, etc. In the second stage, resistance develops. This process, as previously mentioned, was called a "fight or flight" response and first described in 1914 by Dr. Walter Cannon, as an emergency reaction. This process was helpful to ancient man who often needed to prepare for physical action during the hunt or in confrontations with an enemy. However in modern times, these same physiological responses occur regardless of the stressful conditions—most of which are emotional rather than physical. The third stage, "exhaustion", occurs if there is continuous exposure to the same or similar stressors.

It has been known for years that emotional stimuli rank very high among the most potent and prevalent natural stimuli capable of increasing pituitary-adrenal cortical activity. According to Mason in 1968 the unrecognized first mediator in many of Selye's experiments simply may have been the psychological apparatus involved in emotional arousal, which is commonly activated when animals are exposed to "noxious", unpleasant, novel, or arousing conditions.

The previously cited researchers all adhered to a rather narrow definition of stress, ranging from a stimulus definition to an interactive definition. Currently, many persons in the field of stress research have, as opposed to a narrow definition, defined stress in terms of the whole spectrum of interacting factors: stimulus, response and the intervening processes. The intervening processes can be defined as the appraisal of threat, coping styles and social milieu. The R.E.L.A.X. program uses this last definition of stress as a theoretical framework underlying the intended intervention.

Anxiety

One of the negative results of frequent exposure to stress is anxiety. Webster's *New Collegiate Dictionary* defines anxiety as:

> 1: a. painful or apprehensive uneasiness of mind over an impending or anticipated ill; b. fearful concern or interest; c. a cause of anxiety; 2: an abnormal and overwhelming sense of apprehension and fear often marked by physiological signs (as sweating, tension, and increased pulse), by doubt concerning the reality and nature of the threat, and by self-doubt about one's capacity to cope with it.

A review of the literature concluded that anxiety is: 1) elicited by stress, or by threatened deprivation of an anticipated satisfaction; 2) manifested physiologically, phenomenologically, and behaviorally; and 3) is general or situational. They also noted that defensiveness occurs with anxiety and that the consequences of excessive anxiety are usually negative, interfering, and debilitating in nature.

According to James Humphrey, literature on the subject of anxiety as a stress-inducing factor in the educative process reveals the following:

There is a close relation between stress and anxiety.

1. Anxiety is considered a learnable reaction that has the properties of response, a cue of danger, and a drive.
2. Anxiety is internalized fear aroused by the memory of painful past experiences associated with punishment for gratification of an impulse.
3. Anxiety in the classroom interferes with learning, and whatever can be done to reduce it should serve to increase learning.
4. Test anxiety is a near universal experience, especially in

this country, which is a test-giving and test-conscious culture.

5. Evidence from clinical studies points clearly and consistently to the disruptive and distracting power of anxiety effects over most kinds of thinking.

Anxiety has often been defined as fear when there is no physical danger. It is helpful to further delineate anxiety as "general" and "situational".

General and Situational Anxiety

Anxiety is fear when there is no physical danger.

General anxiety, also called trait, chronic, or neurotic anxiety, is a dispositional characteristic. It is a general tendency to be anxious, has an internal locus, and is a result of past experiences. The general tendency to be anxious is often something that has been learned in childhood and brought to adulthood. It becomes a part of one's personality and life style.

Situational anxiety, on the other hand, is a direct function of a particular event. It is specific to an activity, such as talking in front of class, taking a test, or being in a new situation. If excessive, situational anxiety can lead to a phobic reaction. While people who experience this kind of anxiety can become dysfunctional, they usually function without much stress in other areas of their lives.

Adult anxiety was often learned during childhood

It is important to note that anxious feelings are a normal part of life and, at times, are very appropriate. For example, it is normal to experience anxiety in an elevator that is stuck between floors. Likewise, if an examination can affect a person's future, such as admittance to a program or being passed to the next grade level, situational anxiety is the expected norm. When anxiety becomes excessive, however, coping with the situation becomes more difficult.

Anxiety and Success in School

When anxiety becomes excessive, it has been shown to interfere with success in school. O'Reilly and Weghtman found that low-anxious children perform better than high-anxious children on a variety of tasks, including activities such as accurate completion of homework, individual tests, group-ability tests and reading.

Intelligence

General anxiety and scores on intelligence tests have been shown to be negatively correlated. Lighthall, as early as 1959, found that low-anxious children made greater gains over time on the Otis-Lennon Mental Ability Test than high-anxious children. Phillips, Martin, and Meyers studied the relationship between scores on the Children's Manifest Anxiety Scale (CMAS) and IQ scores for 1,200 fifth and sixth grade students. They found a significant negative correlation between high levels of anxiety on the CMAS and IQ scores. Their extensive review of the literature on anxiety in children supported their findings.

Anxiety may cause lower performance on intelligence tests.

There appears to be an even greater negative correlation between test anxiety, or situational anxiety, and scores on IQ tests. This finding was supported in an early literature review by Sarason. It concluded that the majority of studies at that time showed that general anxiety was not related to IQ, whereas high test anxiety was consistently related to poorer performance on IQ tests.

It is important to note that there is good evidence that it is anxiety which causes the lower IQ score and not the reverse. Anxiety does not appear to be a result of low intelligence, however, changes in anxiety level are related to changes in IQ scores. In a longitudinal study of the relationship between anxiety and IQ in a group of 670 elementary school children, Sarason and his colleagues found that increases in anxiety were related to decreases in IQ performance, while decreases in anxiety were related to increases in IQ test performance. Additionally, Sarason, Hill, and Zimardo found that test anxiety affects the more intelligent, as well as average students, by equally affecting their performance on intelligence testing.

Achievement

Research also shows an inverse relationship between anxiety and achievement. Gifford and Marston found that high levels of anxiety were significantly related to slow reading rates and reduced comprehension. Similar results with third grade children were found by Standford, Dember, and Standford. Kahn studied 1,038 eighth-grade students and found that anxiety was a useful predictor of scores on subtests of the Metropolitan Achievement Test. He found that anxiety levels were better predictors of subsequent achievement test results than other predictors, including attitudes and study habits. The negative relationship between anxiety and achievement has also been documented in studies

with seventh-grade children and with fifth and sixth-grade children.

Another study concluded that anxiety was negatively related to school progress, as measured by grades, and suggested that the highly anxious child lacks qualities that make for the productive acquisition and utilization of knowledge. Dendato and Drener also pointed out the negative relationship between anxiety and school success. They found that an intervention program incorporating cognitive relaxation training and study-skills training significantly reduced student's self-reported anxiety and improved their academic performance. Wilson and Rotter's findings in 1986 supported this type of intervention with test-anxious students. D'Alelio and Murrey have demonstrated that cognitive therapies directed toward the reduction of the worry component of test anxiety have been successful in reducing self-reported anxiety. Finally, according to Sarason, several studies indicate that highly anxious children perform poorly on achievement tests because of negative self talk such as "I won't pass," "I'm going to forget the answers," etc. His contention is that their attention to self, rather than to the task, interferes with test performance.

Learning

Anxiety reduces a child's ability to learn.

Research has also shown that test anxiety, in addition to interfering with achievement, was also negatively related to verbal and motor learning, stimulus generalization and size estimation. Ruebush reviewed several studies which showed that anxiety in normal children has negative effects on difficult tasks such as digit symbol and IQ tests. Phillips, Martin, Meyers and Sarason found that when the task is complex, anxiety contributes to more task-irrelevant responses than when the task is simple. In addition to these findings, they noted several other trends. For example, they found that anxiety reduces incidental learning by limiting the perceptual field of the learner. They also reported indications that anxiety negatively affects short-term memory. These reviews of the literature provide consistent evidence of the negative effect of anxiety on a variety of learning tasks and especially on complex learning. In summarizing their findings, they concluded that anxiety is generally debilitating with regard to academic behavior. Spillios and Janzen studied learning disabled children and found that anxiety interfered with their ability to use learning strategies to improve their achievement scores on standardized tests.

Problem Solving

Anxiety generally impairs children's performance on verbal and non-verbal problem-solving tasks. For example, most studies reviewed supported the contention that anxiety interferes with tasks such as mazes and embedded figures and the use of abstract concepts. Several studies also provided evidence that anxiety in children is negatively related to scores on tests of creativity and curiosity.

Sarason, Hill, and Zimardo as early as 1964 studied the effects of anxiety on problem-solving ability in elementary children for IQ, sex and grades. In several problem-solving situations, high-anxious children performed more poorly than low-anxious children. In addition, highly-anxious children tended to be more cautious. Deffenbacher, Michaels and Daley reported similar findings in 1980.

There are several behaviors related to anxiety which interfere with problem-solving ability. Several studies have provided evidence that anxiety reduces responsiveness to the environment and interferes with the accurate perception of reality. Sarason reported that highly anxious children neglect or misinterpret important cues that may be readily available, due to their focus on self, rather than task. In addition, the highly anxious child often experiences attentional blocks.

There are several behaviors related to anxiety which interfere with problem-solving ability.

Dependency

After reviewing the literature, Ruebush reported evidence that excessive anxiety was related to dependence in children. This finding was supported by several other reviews of the literature. Similarly, these reviews reported that direction-seeking and conforming tendencies were related to anxiety.

Rosenthal studied the effects of high and low anxiety on the dependency behavior of three to five year old girls. The children were placed in a strange room with an adult under low- or high-anxiety conditions. The frequency of attention-seeking behavior decreased significantly faster under low-anxiety conditions. Attention-seeking behaviors included attempts to get the adult's attention, praise, or assistance.

Dependency in children may contribute to poor relationships with teachers. For example, dependent children may occupy the teacher's time by asking repeated questions. Finally, according to Sarason, dependence on external authority for approval may be a factor contributing to a lack of creativity in anxious children.

Aggressiveness

One way that anxious students often react is by acting out their aggressive feelings. A significant relationship between school anxiety and hostile, aggressive behavior in school was discovered by Phillips, Martin and Meyers. Thus, it appears that excessive anxiety in children is related to aggressive feelings. Depending on the situation, these aggressive feelings may be expressed outwardly or turned inward.

Self Concept

A consistent positive relationship has been found between excessive anxiety and low self-concept. Several recent studies have found consistent evidence of the relationship between anxiety and two aspects of self-concept: self-disparagement and feelings of inferiority. Excessive anxiety is apparently associated with feelings of guilt, school inadequacy and lack of self-assuredness. These findings were confirmed earlier by Cattel and Sheier. More recently Bellanger and Carter and Russel found that relaxation training improved children's self-report of self-concept.

Excessive anxiety is apparently associated with feelings of guilt, school inadequacy and lack of self-assuredness.

Other Personality Variables

High levels of anxiety in children have been related to a variety of other personality characteristics. Studies have shown that a positive relationship exists between anxiety and various measures of clinical maladjustment. Other personality characteristics affected include dependence, low self-concept, aggression, defensiveness and disturbed relationships with peers and teachers. Additional variables related to high anxiety include indecisiveness, rigidity, cautiousness and guilt. Wesserman noted that children who are anxious often are more prone to symptoms of hypochondria.

Peer Relationships

Several studies have indicated that excessive anxiety is related to low peer status. Hill, for example, studied the effects of anxiety on sociometric status in four third-grade classrooms. He found that high levels of anxiety were related to a negative rela-

Signs of Stress

Following are symptoms of stress often exhibited by children. Any symptom observed as happening often may indicate need for follow up by a teacher, counselor, parent, or physician.

1. Headaches
2. Stomach problems—diarrhea, constipation, nausea, heartburn
3. Heart pounding
4. Aches and pains
5. Muscle jerks or tics
6. Eating problems—no appetite, constant eating, full feeling without eating
7. Sleeping problems—unable to fall asleep, wake up in middle of the night, nightmares
8. General feeling of tiredness
9. Shortness of breath
10. Dry mouth or throat
11. Teeth grinding
12. Stuttering
13. Uncontrollable crying or not being able to cry
14. General anxiety, nervous feelings, or tenseness
15. Dizziness and weakness
16. Irritable and easily set off
17. Depressed
18. Accident prone
19. Feeling angry in general
20. Feeling overwhelmed and unable to cope—wants to run away
21. Nervous laughter, easily startled, jumpy
22. Bored
23. Feeling rejected all the time
24. Unable to concentrate or finish things
25. Never laugh
26. Does not have friends
27. Does not finish homework

Highly anxious children often display attention-seeking behaviors.

tionship between anxiety and accuracy of perception of one's own sociometric status. Flanders and McNamara noted that highly anxious children feel isolated from peers.

Phillips, Martin and Meyers described the following cycle of anxiety and rejection. Isolated and rejected children experience anxiety in social situations. This leads to either less or more activity—acting out or withdrawal. Both are seen as "problem behaviors" by teachers and peers. Although there is an unconscious desire to affiliate when one experiences anxiety, the disruptive or isolated child is usually denied this opportunity and, consequently, experiences more anxiety. Hershey found that children who remained relatively calm in the face of anxiety-laden social situations were better accepted by their peers than those who reacted with a high level of anxiety.

Anxiety and Medical Implications

A holistic approach is needed that takes into consideration both the psychological and physiological aspect of the illness.

Although most physicians would agree that stress and anxiety affect physical health, many are still not aware of the psychological, non-medical literature about stress. Often a physician will treat anxiety with medication, rather than investigate the psychological roots of the problem. At the same time most psychologists refer to the physician to treat organic disease states. This completes a circle that often leaves a child feeling highly anxious. A holistic approach is needed that takes into consideration both the psychological as well as the physiological aspect of the illness. Otherwise a child's anxiety level will complicate nursing care, exacerbate symptoms and in turn create more anxiety for everyone involved.

Anxiety and Brain Research

We know that stress and anxiety cause our adrenal glands to release the peptide called cortisol. This triggers the "flight or fight" response outlined earlier in this chapter. We now know that chronically high cortisol levels lead to the death of brain cells in the hippocampus, which is critical to explicit memory formation. Many recent studies are confirming that both short-term memory and long-term memory are inhibited by stress. We also know that the neurons in the brain of a stressed individual have fewer and shorter dendrites. This deficiency impairs communication with other dendrites. These physical changes in the brain's neural pathways provide added incentive for us to provide children's brains an opportunity for optimal growth. The next three chapters will outline the way this can be accomplished.

3
Methods of Relaxation

The first two chapters established the negative effects of stress and anxiety. The current chapter will focus on research based techniques used to reduce these effects. As mentioned previously, stress, according to Cannon, results when our bodies react in a "fight-or-flight" response. This response is associated with over activity of the sympathetic nervous system. Benson's research indicated a variety of techniques that can be used to "quiet" the aroused sympathetic nervous system.

We all possess a natural mechanism to fight stress.

> Each of us possesses a natural and innate protective mechanism against 'over-stress', which allows us to turn off harmful bodily effects, to counter the effects of the fight-or-flight response. This response against 'over-stress' brings on bodily changes that decrease heart rate, lower metabolism, decrease the rate of breathing, and bring the body back into what is probably a healthier balance. This is the Relaxation Response. (Benson, 1975, pp. 25-26)

Benson suggests that evoking the Relaxation Response is extremely simple if the following four essential elements are included: 1. a quiet environment; 2. a mental device such as a word or a phrase which should be repeated in a specific fashion over and over again; 3. the adoption of a passive attitude; and 4. a comfortable position.

Currently, there are a number of proven techniques that elicit the Relaxation Response. Johnson has shown that various forms of relaxation training have been effective in improving maladaptive behavior and in reducing the effects of stress in children. Based on a literature review, the techniques that were judged by the authors to be least beneficial in a school or home setting include biofeedback, meditation and yoga, hypnosis and systematic desensitization. We felt that biofeedback equipment was too costly and in many instances impractical when working with large groups of children. Hypnosis, meditation and yoga, although highly effective, may be too controversial in many school settings and difficult to learn for parents in the home setting. Systematic desensitization requires trained personnel such as a psychologist, nurse or counselor. We determined that the most effective and easily-administered techniques in a school, medical, or home setting were progressive muscle relaxation, active imagination and music. These techniques are economical, easy to teach, have a high interest level and a solid research base.

Progressive Muscle Relaxation

The technique of progressive muscle relaxation (PMR) was developed by Jacobson in 1944. It is still the technique referred to most often in the literature and probably the one that has had the most widespread application. Yet a recent study by Humphrey revealed that only one percent of teachers surveyed use this technique in their classroom.

In this technique the student concentrates on progressively relaxing one muscle group after another, while comparing the difference between tension and relaxation in each muscle group. The use of PMR is prevalent in the literature as a means of reducing anxiety. Various authors have detailed the exact steps to be followed when using this technique. *Relaxation techniques like PMR have been used to help children become more focused and receptive to subsequent scripts.* Lazarus found that the unconscious mind worked more effectively when subjects were relaxed.

These techniques are economical, easy to teach, have a high interest level and a solid research base.

PMR & Hyperactive Children

According to Chang and Hiebert, PMR at the elementary-school level has been used in the past primarily with children diagnosed as hyperactive and/or having learning and academic problems. These authors cite a number of studies which report encouraging results using PMR as a behavior-management strategy with hyperactive children.

Brown found differential treatment effects between a group of hyperactive elementary school children receiving only PMR and a group receiving PMR plus "task motivational instructions", i.e., instruction in using self-statements that encouraged participation and suggested positive expected outcomes. The combined treatment was significantly more effective than PMR alone in bringing about change on the Davids Rating Scale for Hyperkinesis and the Piers-Harris Self-Concept Scale. Brown concluded that parental support and cognitive strategies are necessary to augment the effects of PMR.

Another study which emphasized the importance of parental involvement in relaxation training was completed by Lupin, Braud, Braud and Derer. They studied the effect of PMR on 13 hyperactive children and their families. Parents received instruction in behavior management and were instructed to listen to PMR tapes, while the children listened to PMR tapes utilizing age-appropriate language. Home practice was assigned and practice data were collected. Parental behavior ratings, Digit Span and Coding subtest scores of the WISC and behavioral observations all indicated significant improvement. Also, frequency of practice was correlated positively with improvement on these dependent measures.

Hyperactive children, as a result of training in PMR, have shown improvement in attention and concentration, behavior and self-concept.

PMR & Learning Problems

Successful results in treating children with learning and academic problems have been obtained by several authors. Padamer used PMR with poor readers in elementary school. Teachers and children in the experimental group received a two-week pretraining, in which conceptual instruction and relaxation practice was given. PMR was then incorporated into the classroom routine. Controls received no training. Experimental subjects demonstrated improved reading achievement while controls did not. Spillios and Janzen studied the effects of PMR on anxious learning-disabled children, and found that highly-anxious children improved under the relaxation condition, but the medium and low-anxiety children remained unchanged.

PMR & Regular Learners

Preventative PMR programs with normal populations have been tested only recently when compared to other PMR research. The majority of these studies have been done at the secondary level. One of the few studies at the elementary level was one completed by Zaichkowsky and Zaichkowsky. They evaluated PMR with 24 fourth-grade children who received 18 lessons of 10 to 20 minutes. Home practice was encouraged but not logged. Experimental subjects improved significantly on measures of skin temperature, respiration, heart rate and state anxiety. Experimental subjects differed significantly from control subjects on heart rate and respiration rate at post-test.

Active Imagination

The use of active imagination by psychologists has been making a comeback in popularity during the past two decades. Psychologists and others have long noted the mind's ability to mimic internally the possible motions and transformations of objects in the external world.

The key concept of active imagination is the belief that when people imagine themselves successfully performing a certain behavior, the likelihood for taking part in that behavior increases.

The power of this technique was noted as early as the 1700's by David Hume who wrote that to "join incongruous shapes and appearances costs the imagination no more trouble than to conceive the most natural and familiar objects....This creative power of the mind amounts to no more than the faculty of comprehending, transposing, augmenting, or diminishing the material afforded us by the senses and experience."

The study of active imagination has always been a part of the science of the mind. However, it has been referred to in different ways. During the dominance of Watson and behaviorism, it was studied as "conditioned hallucinations" (Selye, 1956, p. 14). According to Yuille acceptance of active imagination as a field of legitimate research was not apparent until the 1960's. Ulric Neisser chose active imagination as the topic when addressing the first conference of the City University's Center for Research in Cognition and Affect in New York City in June, 1967. Since the conference of 1967 was held, there has been a steadily increasing amount of research relating to the use of imagination.

FUNKY WINKERBEAN   **by Tom Batiuk**

The key concept of active imagination is the belief that when people imagine themselves successfully performing a certain behavior, the likelihood for taking part in that behavior increases. Research has supported this concept. Active imagination has also been shown to reduce depression, build positive attitudes and reduce anxiety. A number of studies have indicated that active imagination is capable of influencing attitudes, feelings and behavior.

Active imagination is an essential component of a primary prevention school-based program because of its reliance on teaching children the use of positive self-talk.

Recently, Speidel and Troy encouraged researchers to explore the beneficial effects of active imagination in helping children cope with everyday problems. There is evidence to suggest that children are less able than adults to discriminate imagined actions from performed actions. This would imply that children may be more responsive than adults to the effects of active imagination. Active imagination in the form of guided fantasies can promote a feeling of calmness, as well as being a stimulus for self-exploration or creative imagination.

Suzuki found implications for education from learning theory research which has been conducted on children's imagination. Active imagination was identified as a strategy used in learning and remembering. Suzuki's research suggests that imagination elaboration-prompting (e.g., Imagine that A and B are...) facilitates learning, including the learning of tasks closely resembling school tasks.

Mental practice can be described as symbolic rehearsal of a physical activity in the absence of any gross muscular movement. The use of mental practice in performing motor skills is not new since research efforts have been occurring for more than half a century. The research has demonstrated that imagining a movement reproduces recordable electric-action potentials from the muscle groups that would actually carry out the movement. Thus, mental rehearsal under conditions of relaxation has grown in popularity and has created an awareness, especially in athletic circles, that active imagination can be a useful technique.

Self-Talk

One procedure in the use of mental practice for relaxation is that of making suggestions to one's self. Humphrey, in his book *Stress in Childhood* states that "... as children we first learn to act on the basis of verbal instructions from others" (p. 42). As early as 1959, Luria indicated that we learn to direct our own behavior on the basis of our own language activities. This point of view suggests that speech as a form of communication between children and adults later becomes the way a child organizes his/her own behavior. In 1986, Brown, O'Keefe, Sanders and Baker found

Athletes use success active imagination to improve performance.

Active imagination techniques using self-talk have been used to positively alter self-perceptions, as well as expectations and behaviors.

that positive self-talk in children was the most frequently reported cognitive coping strategy. These authors found, however, that only a small percentage of children reported using such strategies. *Active imagination is an essential component of a primary prevention school-based program because of its reliance on teaching children the use of positive self-talk.* It is likely that many children do not engage in positive self-talk simply because the significant others in their lives have not provided the necessary verbal modeling, nor have the schools taught them how to use this technique.

The importance of implementing programs to teach children how to use positive self-talk is indicated by our literature review. For example, according to one study, 79% of 8- to 9-year-olds tend to exaggerate perceived negative aspects of a stressful situation, make denigrating self-statements and/or have thoughts of escape or avoidance. Brown and O'Keefe used the term "catastrophizing" to define the coping strategy of this population of children. The fact that catastrophizing occurred at such a high rate was itself of concern, as well as the fact that it seemed to make an already stressful situation worse. It follows, then, that if a child has a tendency to catastrophize in a variety of different situations, he will probably also be more anxious in general than peers who cope in a variety of situations. Coping was defined broadly as the imagining of events that are inconsistent with the experience of pain or stress, thinking about objects in the environment, stopping oneself from thinking of the pain/stress, talking to oneself (or someone else) in such a way as to minimize pain/stress and thinking about the stressful event in a problem-solving way.

Several researchers have reported success in using active imagination as an aspect of relaxation with children. They found that this technique was more successful in eliminating off-task behavior than traditional behavior-management techniques. Additionally, they noted improvement in attitude and achievement. McBrien, in his work with first graders, used the following instructions involving the use of imagination:

> Just imagine you are lying on your back on soft green grass . . .
> you are so comfortable as you look up through the branches
> and leaves of a shade tree at the deep blue sky . . . you can see
> soft, white, puffy clouds floating by.

The importance of positive self-talk is essential.

Further instructions to focus on the pleasant feeling of relaxation would then follow. Another way active imagination has been used to promote a relaxed state is by using comparative statements such as "float like a feather" or "melt like snow".

The self-concept or self-image serves the function of organizing and guiding behavior. Active imagination techniques using self-talk have been used to positively alter self-perceptions, as well as expectations and behaviors.

To summarize, active imagination and positive self-talk have been used successfully to promote creativity and feelings of calmness among elementary age children. *The importance of positive self-talk is essential in improving self-concept, skill building and improvement of behavior, attitude, and achievement.*

Music

According to Ostrander and Schroeder, the ancient schools of music believed that music was the bridge linking all things. Following the ideas of Pythogoras, they built a "sacred canon of specific harmonies, intervals and proportions into their music. Such ideas were used by the composers of Baroque music. Musicians in those eras were trained and required to use these particular numbers and patterns for harmony, counterpoint, rhythm and tempo in their music. Thus, Baroque music was supposed to affect the listener by aligning, harmonizing and synchronizing mind and body to more harmonious patterns.

Music, such as Baroque, has been found effective in stress reduction as measured by physiological changes. Some of the physiological measures of music's effects on anxiety/stress reduction include galvanic skin response, heart rate, pulse rate and blood pressure, respiration rate, EMG and the EEG. Shifts in mood and attitude as a function of music were also documented as early as 1921 by Gatewood. Recently, Wesecky suggests that the reactivity for rhythm and melodies must be located within a primitive region of the hierarchical structure of the brain, because even severely retarded children respond to music. He demonstrated that music therapy can bring about at least a temporary cessation of the stereotyped movements in children with Rett syndrome. Cratty found improvement in self-help skills of retarded children after using relaxation exercises accompanied by relaxing music.

In a review of the entire class of music, Logan stressed the importance of selecting the right piece of music to ensure the success of an experiment. One of the more difficult problems was how to resolve the selection of "soft and relaxing" music as the term itself creates an ambiguous variable. An important factor in music selection is the intended subjects' report of liking the music.

In the mid-1960's, Lozanor and Balevsky used background classical music to enhance learning. About that time, a California researcher, Dorothy Retallack found that plants grown in chambers where Baroque music by Bach and Indian music by Ravi Shankar were played grew more rapidly and lush than plants exposed to other types of music (jazz, country, rock) or those without music.

Calming music has been found to enhance relaxation and learning, reduce heart and respiration rates, and aid in the effectiveness of other relaxation techniques.

In summary, relaxing music has been found to enhance relaxation and learning, reduce heart and respiration rate, and aid the effectiveness of other relaxation techniques. It can be applied easily to large groups and allows children to gain an appreciation of a type of music not often heard in the home setting.

Music Selections

The music listed below was used with the original research and has been very popular with the children. It was purposely chosen as being particularly relaxing. This music is available for purchase on compact disk by sending a check, purchase order, or money order to: Inner Coaching 1108 Western Avenue, Watertown, Wisconsin 53094. All of the materials below can be ordered by using the form at the end of this book.

Pianoscapes (Jones) - Soothing Piano Solos.
Language of Love (Lamb) - Music for classrooms, offices, or hospitals.
Pachelbel w/ Ocean (Liv & Let Liv) - Cannon D soundscapes.
Bach Forever by the Sea (Gibson) -Ten classics with sounds of the sea.
The Fairy Ring (Rowland)- Music on piano/synthesizer.

Other Inner Coaching Products

Ready, Set, Release (Klein & Allen) – Music and relaxation exercises. This 74-minute tape/CD offers 14 fun and calming exercises using music, breathing, muscle relaxation and guided active imagination to soothe and release tension. This companion (or stand alone) piece to Ready, Set, R.E.L.A.X., has proven effective for children from preschool to middle school. ISBN 0-9636027-1-3

Relaxation and Success Imagery (Klein & Klein) - Muscle relaxation, positive statements and original background music for teenagers and adults (tape only).

Healing Images for Children (Nancy Klein) - Teaching relaxation and guided imagery to children facing cancer and other serious illnesses. A guide for families and health care providers with educational information relating to medical treatments and relaxation strategies. ISBN 0-9636027-2-1

Healing Images for Children CD (Klein & Klein) - Seven stories, 70 minutes, with musical background to reinforce techniques from the book Healing Images for Children. ISBN 0-9636027-3 -X

Healing Images for Children Activity Book (Klein) - Ninety pages of coloring, drawing, playing and writing for days when quiet activities are best. ISBN 0-9636027-4-8

The Kid's Wellness Guide (Voght & Holden) - This 160 page program brings long recognized body/mind practices to young children ages 3 to 6 as it links their physically expressive bodies to their active imaginations. ISBN 0-9662340-1-4

4
Intervention Strategies

Attitudes and perceptions of self are formed early in life and remain with us throughout our lives as memory traces and influences of our behavior. This suggests that adults must do everything possible to ensure that children have an opportunity to develop positive attitudes and perceptions of themselves. Children who are given positive messages at home would benefit from reinforcement of those messages at school, while children who receive negative messages at home need exposure to positive messages. Skill in stress management is also an important factor in a child's personal development. Several studies have found a significant change in attentiveness of children when relaxation training was used. Other studies have shown that various measures of anxiety can be lowered as a result of the use of relaxation procedures or active imagination.

However, very little work has been done in applying these techniques with large groups of children. Most research deals with the treatment of a single child or a few children. This is especially true when the techniques include a biofeedback component. Carter and Russel's research in 1982 was done with five or six children at a time. Although they reported significant treatment effects using biofeedback, they concluded that classroom teachers were unable to duplicate this effect. They agreed that the teachers never became comfortable with the biofeedback machinery. The teachers did quite well, however, in assisting the children in listening to relaxation tapes.

Perhaps one of the factors that has limited research with large groups of children has been the requirement of relatively large blocks of time for teacher training and program implementation. For the procedures to be successful they must be understood easily by children and able to be delivered to a large group. There should be minimal time loss from the teaching day and, if pos-

Attitudes and perceptions of self are formed early in life and remain with us throughout our lives as memory traces and influences of our behavior.

sible, the entire school population should have the opportunity to be included in the training. For optimal impact, anti-stress practices should be included in everyday school routines. Contrary to these recommendations, the majority of studies reviewed dealt with relatively small groups.

The school setting is a natural delivery system for a preventative mental health program. The healthy development of children involves coping successfully with stressful experiences. When children are under stress, even high levels of stress, but have strong social supports, they exhibit fewer symptoms of anxiety than do children with less support. An important component of the child's social system is the school. A system-wide intervention program impacts on this social system, and thus provides a greater impact on each individual.

Cauce, Comer and Schwartz in a study determined that the long-term effects of a systems-oriented school prevention program were positive. This was an important finding, as prior to this study short-term effects of preventative efforts were reasonably well established, but it was unclear whether these efforts had detectable long-term effects.

The literature reviewed supported the idea of a relatively long program as opposed to the introduction of relaxation training in a short time frame. Better relaxation treatment effects were shown when the program was at least six weeks in length.

Relaxation programs have improved student's achievement scores, decreased levels of anxiety, increased self-concept and demonstrated children's ability to regulate heart rate, respiration rate and skin temperature.

Program Delivery

Another important factor in determining success rate is how the program is delivered. Because of the techniques involved and/or standardization requirements for research, many of the researchers were directly involved. Herzog maintained that children appear more able to relax in an environment that does not include strangers. Therefore, a program delivered by someone familiar to the child should yield more optimal results.

Gerber and Danilson's study was one of the few with a large number of subjects. Sixteen school counselors received training and instruction on the theory and use of the quieting reflex (QR) and of success imagery (SI) which was developed in 1980 by Holland, Stroebel and Stroebel. This two-phase study demonstrated that a given visualization strategy (SI), when used in combination with a given relaxation technique (QR), can help students minimize the debilitating effects of anxiety and stress and increase their scores on a standardized test, specifically the Science Research Associates Achievement Test.

The application of relaxation techniques has been successful in school-based intervention programs. These programs have improved student's achievement scores, decreased levels of anxiety, increased self-concept and demonstrated children's ability to regulate bodily functions (heart rate, respiration rate, and skin temperature). Programs of relatively long duration (greater than six weeks) and implemented by persons familiar to the children appear to be most beneficial.

Origins of the Ready, Set, R.E.L.A.X. Program

The call for a school-based program designed to help children reduce anxiety is clearly supported in the literature. School-based special services providers need to implement stress management education programs if optimal learning and development are to occur. Our interest in a school-based program developed over the last ten years. It began with a stress-reduction program we designed for high school varsity athletes. Progressive muscle relaxation, active imagination and music were presented during ten weekly sessions. Pre- and post-testing using self-report inventories showed statistically significant results in decreasing anxiety and depression and increasing self-concept. Following this program, the authors used the same methods in an attempt to increase the musical skills of high school student-band participants. Ten weekly sessions were held during which time the experimental group was led through a relaxation, active imagination exercise. Although musical performance, as measured by the Watkins-Farnum Music Performance Test, did not differ significantly from control-group students, self-report inventories of anxiety and depression generally decreased while self-reported self-concept increased. The participants in both these groups frequently stated that the techniques used would be beneficial to all students. This feedback, coupled with the knowledge of the damaging effects of stress and anxiety in children, led the authors to consider a school-wide intervention program. The concept of a primary prevention program was appealing from the standpoint of the potential to have a positive impact on a large number of children. There is a critical need for stress management programs at all levels of education. The goal of the program was to provide a tool for children to use in a variety of settings to combat the negative effects of stress and anxiety.

The elementary school level was chosen for several reasons. First, this age child tends to be more receptive to new experiences and would be more likely to be a cooperative subject. Second, the school schedule is more flexible than in a secondary school setting and lends itself to an available block of time for a school-wide intervention. Finally, the hope was to provide a pro-

There is a critical need for stress management programs at all levels of education.

The goal of the program was to provide a tool for children to use in a variety of settings to combat the negative effects of stress and anxiety.

An additonal benefit of the program is that children will develop an appreciation of enriching music.

gram that students would incorporate into their daily lives throughout the year.

Currently, to our knowledge, there is no systematic program in existence that exposes children to stress-reduction techniques over a long period of time. The longest program noted in the literature was Disorbio's, which spanned a six-month period. A program over an extended period of time is more likely to be incorporated into a child's lifestyle. A school or teacher that makes such a commitment of time sends an important message to children that affective education is an essential component of the total education program.

Multi-Method Advantages

In the Ready, Set, R.E.L.A.X. (R.S.R.) program, the use of relaxing music was used as an adjunct to muscle relaxation and active imagination. Interestingly, no other reports of combining the three techniques of music, active imagination and muscle relaxation are reported in the literature. Not only is the use of such music supported by research, but the authors' experience using music with their own children and with students in school, at workshops and in groups gave evidence of its benefits. Children who do not actively take part in the progressive muscle relaxation or active imagination are at least exposed to a passive form of relaxation. An additional benefit is the opportunity to develop an appreciation for an enriching form of music.

One of the values of using a multi-method intervention is based on Folkman's 1985 research indicating that each person has his/her own individual style of seeing the world. For some people, change is accomplished through behavior, which in turn affects cognition and feeling. For others, the key to change is through cognition, which in turn affects feelings and behavior.

FUNKY WINKERBEAN

Theoretically, then, some students may benefit more directly from the use of progressive muscle relaxation while others may benefit more from a cognitive-based success active imagination technique. People usually use several types of coping behavior in virtually every type of stressful encounter. This includes coping that is directed at solving or managing the problem that is causing distress (problem-focused coping) and coping that is directed at regulating the distress itself (emotion-focused coping) . Thus, it is important to try to teach children how to select the most appropriate mode of coping. For example, if a problem is not solvable (disliking someone's personality), continuing to engage in problem-focused behavior becomes counter productive. Likewise, the same is true for engaging in emotion-focused coping when direct action and problem solving will resolve the conflict. Therefore, an important component of any intervention program is teaching children how to realistically appraise what must be done in a specific situation. The Ready, Set, R.E.L.A.X. program provides this component by having the students imagine themselves resolving problem-oriented issues. Additionally, suggestions are given to the classroom teacher for a brief follow-up discussion of the topic for the day. Other follow-up activities and projects are available. Also included in the R. S. R. program is an opportunity for the students to repeat a positive self-statement. The purpose of these self-statements is to have the students develop a problem-solving response set. Self regulated, private speech can function as an instructional cue that guides one's thoughts, feelings and behaviors. It has been demonstrated that self-instructions have an influence on one's appraisal, attentional processes and physiological reactions. Stress management procedures can be effective only when they stimulate new ways of appraising potentially stressful conditions and coping with them.

It is important to try to teach children the most appropriate mode of coping.

12 Tips to Relieve Stress for Children and Adults

When you get that "stressed out" feeling, why not try:

1. Deep breathing/Muscle Relaxation
2. Meditating/Praying
3. Listening to relaxing music, or your favorite music
4. Exercising (stretch, walk, run, swim, bike)
5. Playing with your pet
6. Closing your eyes and recalling a fond memory
7. Developing a sense of humor
8. Expressing feelings
9. Eating healthy food
10. Making a list to help yourself get organized
11. Taking a warm bath
12. Making time to have fun

Remember, some stress is a fact of life. How we respond to stressful situations in our lives is up to us. Will we control the stress or will stress control us?

5
Ready, Set, R.E.L.A.X. Research

Program Goals

The Ready, Set, R.E.L.A.X. program is unique in the field because of its research base. Many books, programs and scripts are available on the market today but few, if any, offer any solid research to back their claims. The R.E.L.A.X. program was analyzed using a traditional research paradigm.

    The goals of the R.S.R. program are:

- to help children understand the role of anxiety and relaxation in their lives.
- to help children become more aware of the feelings associated with tension and relaxation.
- to help children become more aware of their bodies and the physical manifestations of stress.
- to help children identify situations where stress and anxiety are often present.
- to help children learn, through experience, skills and techniques, that will help them relax and reduce tension.
- to encourage children to practice the skills daily.
- to help children identify how these skills might be applied at appropriate times in their lives.
- to help children develop a problem-solving response set.
- to help children develop an appreciation for Baroque and other relaxing music.
- to help children develop positive self-talk skills.

Subjects

The experimental subjects in the pilot year of the R.E.L.A.X. Program were 123 first through sixth grade students enrolled in a parochial school in a small midwestern rural community of 20,000, primarily of middle to lower-middle income status. The subjects were predominately white, all had female teachers and represented the portion of the enrollment of the school that remained stable over two years.

The control group subjects were 120 students enrolled in another parochial grade school in the same community. These subjects were predominately white, had female teachers and represented the entire enrollment of the school that remained stable over two years. Children in both schools were similar in chronological age, intelligence, as measured by the cognitive index of the Metropolitan Achievement Test, and socioeconomic level, as assessed by the Hollingshead Two Factor Index of Social Position. The subjects during the second year of the study remained the same with the exception of an additional set of first grade students and graduation of sixth grade students .

The success of the Ready, Set, R.E.L.A.X. program is documented by solid research.

Materials

There were six main types of materials used:

1. Pre- and post-testing was completed using various self-report inventories. Children in Grades 1–3 were administered the Revised Children's Manifest Anxiety Scale and the Depression Inventory for Children, while children in Grades 4–6 were administered the Revised Children's Manifest Anxiety Scale and the Piers-Harris Children's Self Concept Scale.
2. A series of original active imagination and progressive muscle-relaxation scripts (See Part II).
3. An introductory letter to introduce the program to parents (See Appendix A).
4. Inservice programs for staff, students and parents (See Appendices B, C, D).
5. Music selections, including Baroque classics as well as other relaxing music (See page 28).
6. A questionnaire to obtain feedback from students in the R.E.L.A.X. program (See Appendix E).

Procedure

To obtain permission to implement the program, an overview of the program was presented to the school board of each of the targeted schools for their formal endorsement. After school-board approval, a letter explaining the program was sent to each parent (Appendix A). An inservice program was then held with the faculty of the experimental school to explain data-gathering procedures and to provide an introduction to the R.E.L.A.X. program and materials (Appendix B) Then a parent inservice was held to discuss stress and answer any questions about the program (Appendix D) This was followed by pretesting during the second week of school using the Revised Children's Manifest Anxiety Scale (RCMAS), the Depression Inventory for Children and the Piers-Harris Children's Self-Concept Scale Students in grades one through three were given the RCMAS and the Depression Inventory. Teachers at these levels were asked to read the items to their students and define unfamiliar words. Students in grades four through six were asked to complete the RCMAS and the Self-Concept Scale. Teachers in these grades monitored the testing and answered questions or defined words as needed. The same instruments were administered and the same instructions were used with all students grades one through six in the control-group school.

Next, a workshop was presented to the experimental school students in order to give factual information about stress and lead them in discussion about its psychological and physiological effects (Appendix C). The R.S.R. program was explained to the students by the principal and the group was led through a relaxation experience.

The R.S.R. program was implemented during the fourth week of school and ran through April of the following spring. During the first month, first through third graders listened to R.S.R. scripts on Monday, Wednesday and Friday from 12:45 p.m. to 1:00 p.m., while fourth through sixth graders listened on Tuesday, Wednesday and Thursday at the same time. On non-RSR days a silent reading time was given while music played.

The scripts were read over the intercom by the school principal. The R.E.L.A.X. session was introduced by stating, "Boys and girls it is time for Ready, Set, R.E.L.A.X.", which was followed by two minutes of the music selection. While the music played the classroom teachers turned off the classroom lights and instructed their students to clear their desks, place their feet flat on the floor, place their hands on their thighs, bow their heads slightly forward and close their eyes. At the end of the two minutes, the principal began reading the script while the music continued in the background.

Everything you need to successfully use this program is in this book.

"Boys and girls it is time for Ready, Set, R.E.L.A.X."

At the end of the script each teacher led the class in a brief discussion using the questions provided at the end of each script.

In the second year of the study, test preparation scripts were also read each day for one week preceding administration of the Metropolitan Achievement Tests. Initially scripts were read three times a week (M, W, F) in an effort to help students achieve proficiency in obtaining a relaxation response. After October, R.S.R. scripts were read only twice a week with sustained silent reading on the other three days. Other than the pre- and post-testing, nothing out of the normal routine occurred at the control school.

The procedure during the pilot year differed in several ways. First, all grade levels listened to the same scripts on the same days. Second, there was no follow-up discussion, which became one of the more valuable opportunities to integrate the R.S.R. messages during the second year. Third, no test preparation scripts were available. The hope during the second year was to increase students' overall performance on the Metropolitan Achievement Tests by using relaxation and active imagination prior to the students completing the testing.

As a group, the test students demonstrated decreased anxiety and depression and increased self-concept and achievement.

Conclusions of Study

Based on the results of the statistical analysis of the data gathered, several general conclusions can be drawn. First, children in the experimental group (receiving the intervention) showed statistically significant benefits when compared to their matched controls. As a group, they demonstrated decreased anxiety and depression and increased self-concept and achievement. Second, within-group comparisons suggest a "cumulative" effect of the program, with more significant changes occurring at post-testing during the second year. Third, achievement test results increased as reported levels of anxiety decreased. Fourth, the stability of post-test results from the first year, when compared to pre-test results from the second year, support the usefulness of the chosen self-report inventories and suggest children's self perceptions in grades one through six were relatively stable over a four-month period. For a detailed analysis of these results please write the authors (in care of the publisher.)

The Ready, Set, R.E.L.A.X. program provides an economical and easily implemented procedure that can be used with various-sized groups of children The intent was to provide a program that would be used school-wide on an annual basis. However, the program is easily adaptable for use with individual or small groups of children.

The R.S.R. program was designed to be more than the mere exposure of children to taped relaxation scripts.

The R.S.R. program was designed to be more than the mere exposure of children to taped relaxation scripts. Such procedures without the context of purposeful, guided instruction have been shown through research to be ineffective. Instruction providing students with a clear, age-appropriate theoretical basis, and emphasizing transfer of learning seems to be most helpful. The R.S.R. program makes special effort to provide such instruction through the "inservice" training of staff, parents and children. Additionally, positive self-talk is encouraged and solidified through discussion with the facilitator after each R.S.R. session. Every teacher in the experimental school was enthusiastic and supportive of the program. The positive effects of adult praise and reinforcement on the children's willingness to participate has frequently been reported in the literature. In a study by Day, a clear training outcome was evident, but eroded after the cessation of in-class practice, indicating the importance of structuring some long-term, follow-up practice.

Teachers, counselors, nurses, physicians, social workers and psychologists are frequently placed in a situation of "putting out fires" rather than preventing them. The R.S.R. program is an attempt to prevent future fires by equipping young children to manage feelings of anxiety. Further longitudinal research is needed to determine if the R.S.R. program has beneficial effects once a student no longer practices in a structured setting. Additionally, it is hoped this effort will encourage others to use the R.S.R. program to verify the obtained results. "Mental health" is an important commodity which necessitates that all those in the helping professions expend more energy in well-grounded, research-based prevention programs.

Helping professionals are frequently placed in a situation of "putting out fires" rather than preventing them.

6
Using Ready, Set, R.E.L.A.X.

Using The Program in Your Setting

Your next step is to determine how to best use Ready, Set, R.E.L.A.X. in your setting. *Although the research emphasized the use of R.S.R. as a school wide intervention, it is easily adaptable to use with individuals, small groups, a single classroom, a hospital or clinic setting and at home.*

It is important to read the scripts at a slow pace in somewhat of a monotone voice. This pacing is necessary to give children enough time to maintain relaxation and form mental images while the monotone voice helps promote relaxation. You will notice that each R.S.R. script begins with the same phrase. The opening is intended to act as an anchor and aide the child's ability to concentrate on the main body of the script. Both the music and the ability to relax help the child focus and block out interfering thoughts. Thus the two minute run of music and the introductory comments and suggestions to relax are important ingredients to a successful experience. Before you play the music remind the children that R.S.R. is about to begin. *You will want to set the mood for relaxation by dimming the lights and actually slowing down your talking and body language.* The more relaxed you are the easier it will be for the children to relax. Suggestions for relaxing music are included in Chapter 3 and are available for purchase by contacting the authors or completing the order form at the end of the book.

We suggest you review the first section of this book to be certain that you have a good understanding of the original R.S.R. research and the methods used by the authors to implement the program. Although the research was based on using the program on a regular basis throughout the year, the scripts certainly lend themselves to periodic use to support various topics you may want to emphasize.

Ready, Set, R.E.L.A.X. is adaptable to use with individuals, small groups, a single classroom, a hospital or clinic setting and at home.

Program Themes

The main themes of the scripts are releasing tension (R), enjoyment (E), learning (L), appreciation of self and others (A) and expanding feelings to other situations (X). Within these themes are choices to emphasize particular subjects such as self-esteem, creativity, peer pressure or special days and seasons. A series of test preparation scripts included in the Learn section were used in the original research to help students prepare for the Metropolitan Achievement Tests. They are easily adaptable for use in a variety of testing situations. Other story scripts in the Learn section also deal with test anxiety.

Within these themes are choices to emphasize particular subjects such as self-esteem, creativity, peer pressure or special days and seasons.

All scripts are intended to evoke vivid images which help solidify the main theme of each exercise. You will notice that the children are asked to repeat the main theme three times. The visual picture and "story" is intended to elicit an emotional response. This response increases the probability of the message being retained by the children. You may want to repeat certain scripts a number of times to emphasize a theme you feel is particularly important. Every time an image is repeated there is potential for new emotional responses which will help the child remember the intended message. A cross reference section is included in this book on pages 48 and 49 to help you match particular themes to the needs of your children. The reader is also encouraged to adapt the scripts to meet the individual needs of the children involved. For example, some rural and urban children may have a different frame of reference for certain images. After the release section has been practiced, the scripts can be used in any order and adapted to meet the needs for your situation.

If the relaxation techniques are being used in a medical setting or at home or school with children who have serious medical conditions, the child's primary physician should be informed so that the relaxation can be accounted for in the overall treatment program. For example, having a diabetic child relax after strenuous physical activity may lower the blood sugar to an unwanted level if not monitored and planned for in the treatment regime.

Getting Ready to Relax

Emphasize to the children that relaxation is enjoyable and allows them to be more open to learning. Assure them that they are totally in control of this learning. They are not being hypnotized or "duped" by some magical process. They may choose to alter a particular image to one which is more familiar to them. *Encourage the children to keep their eyes closed during the R.S.R. exercise.* This eliminates many of the distractions which might break their concentration. Although eyes closed is the preferred method, some children may feel more comfortable with their eyes open. Not all children will actively take part in the exercises. We found that approximately 17% of children in our sample did not actively participate. Again the choice to participate or not is an individual matter. However, you will need to emphasize the importance of everyone remaining quiet during the reading of the scripts.

Some children prefer laying their heads on their desks or lying down while listening. A body position that seems to promote relaxation if sitting consists of having the child place both feet flat on the floor, hands on thighs and head bent slightly forward with the chin almost resting on the chest. If laying on the floor, a small pillow under the neck and knees with arms and hands resting next to the body is suggested.

There is no particular time of day that is "best" to use R.S.R. scripts. If using the program at home, the music and script will allow a natural transition to sleep and would add to the value of the child's established bedtime routine. This could be could be especially helpful to children who have a difficult time relaxing. Within the school setting, some teachers prefer having R.S.R. time following recess or gym. They report that their students seem better able to transition into doing cognitive tasks afterward. Others have found R.S.R. to be a nice right brain activity after a cognitive left brain task. If using the program on a school-wide basis, consensus needs to be reached as to what is best for the majority of the teachers. Regardless of the time chosen we encourage you to provide a sustained silent reading opportunity in the same time slot on the days R.S.R. is not used. The frequency of reading scripts is your choice. We began the year with scripts three times a week for the first two months and two times the remainder of the school year. As already mentioned, repetition of scripts can be valuable. Children seem to choose their favorite ones and look forward to hearing particular scripts. The cumulative effect of using this program throughout a child's years in primary school can not be over emphasized.

The length of the exercise will vary depending on the follow up discussion and whether or not you choose to do a follow up activity. Initially the progressive muscle relaxation exercises will only be about ten minutes long. *The scripts included in the Release section entitled "progressive muscle relaxation" (PMR 1- PMR 7) are an important basis for establishing a child's ability to achieve a relaxation response.* For the remaining scripts a time slot of fifteen to twenty minutes is suggested. The choice to use a follow up activity may depend on how well it fits into some of your ongoing lessons or individual needs.

Children have an uncanny ability to use their imagination. Research has shown nearly all children have the capability to see

Using the discussion questions and activities reinforces learning and extends the fun.

Nearly all children have the capability to see vivid images.

vivid images. Children are much more in "practice" than adults because of their natural ability to daydream and use fantasy in their daily play. The R.S.R. program capitalizes on this gift of active imagination and provides a springboard for positive change. We welcome your feedback and are available to provide inservice training, music recommendations or further background information. Call us at 920-262-0439 or write to us at the following address: Inner Coaching, 1108 Western Avenue, Watertown, Wisconsin, 53094. Email: kids@readysetrelax.com. Visit our web site for current information: www.readysetrelax.com

You are ready and set, now RELAX and enjoy the rest of the book!

Part II

The Ready, Set, R.E.L.A.X. Program Scripts

Ready, Set, R.E.L.A.X. Facilitator's Guide

The following scripts help children use active imagination to enhance academic and behavioral skills. By adding music, relaxation techniques, positive affirmations and follow up questions and activities, this program can be an exciting addition to your interaction with children.

When To Use Ready, Set, R.E.L.A.X.

Ready, Set, R.E.L.A.X. scripts can be used almost any time of the day. Use it in the following situations:

1. To lessen the effect of stress with planned intervention.
2. To relax children after a strenuous activity.
3. To help children calm down after conflict.
4. To teach children to use breathing and PMR.
5. To teach children to enjoy alternative types of music.
6. To improve school performance.
7. To help children stay calm in tense situations.
8. To help combat test anxiety.
9. To encourage creative writing.
10. To practice listening skills.
11. To relax after a busy day or prepare for sleep.
12. To encourage positive thinking.
13. To focus concentration.
14. To develop a positive self concept.
15. To practice using the imagination.
16. To have "fun".

Organization of R.E.L.A.X. Scripts

The program scripts are divided into five main areas:

R. Release scripts emphasize breathing & muscle relaxation to open the mind and senses.
E. Enjoy scripts focus on using the creative imagination to feel good about oneself.
L. Learn scripts stress opening the mind to academic motivation and success.
A. Appreciate scripts reinforce a healthy self concept and relationships with others.
X. X-pand scripts take the concepts of R.E.L.A.X. and apply them to other real life experiences.

You should begin the Ready, Set, R.E.L.A.X. program with the Release relaxation exercises; then continue with the scripts in sequence, or pick and choose to meet specific goals or needs. There is a cross reference grid on pages 48 and 49. The positive affirmations are listed in the table of contents next to the title of the scripts.

Using the Scripts — Tips For The Facilitator

The setting for the facilitation of the R.E.L.A.X. scripts will vary according to your situation and age of population. The following are a few general guidelines that will help prepare children for the program.

1. Dim the lights (if possible) and calmly ask the children to get ready for the Ready, Set, R.E.L.A.X. program.
2. Soft background music should begin (see page 28 for selections).
3. Ask children to close their eyes and find a comfortable position. They may drop their head slightly, rest their head or their arms on their desk, or even lay on their back, if space permits. (See Chapter 6 for more details.)
4. Begin each script by reading the warm up section with a calm, rhythmic, monotone voice.
5. Continue reading the script at an even pace, pause frequently.
6. You may choose to use the discussion questions and activities provided or develop follow up options of your own.
7. Scripts can be repeated or slightly modified.

We hope you relax, enjoy, learn from, appreciate and x-pand your usage of Ready, Set, R.E.L.A.X.

Cross Reference of Major Topics

	Progressive Muscle Relax.	Breathing	Self-Esteem	Creativity	Testing	Academics	Imagination	Seasons/Nature	Positive Thinking	Senses	Growing/Changing	Motivation	Sharing	Peer Pressure	Acceptance	Health
RELEASE (pp. 61–77)																
Body Breathing	•	•														
Push and Relax	•															
Breath in, Breath out		•	•													
Letting Go	•	•					•									
Rainbow Walking							•			•						
Wash Away Tension	•	•						•		•						
Stairway to Relax.		•								•						
Cloud of Calmness		•	•				•									
Solar Energy	•			•												
Rolling Waves	•	•								•						
Color Connecting				•				•								
Big Balloon		•					•									
ENJOY (pp. 80–100)																
Toy Store Trip							•									
Fall Fireworks								•		•						
Popcorn Fun							•									
The Complete Meal										•			•			
A Little Adventure	•			•			•									
Airborne			•				•				•					
Candy Store		•								•		•				
Bouncing Ball								•								
Hidden Heros			•												•	
Bicycle Trip	•	•	•				•									
Star Gazing				•												
LEARN (pp. 104–125)																
Rainbow Wear	•				•		•									
Bubble Blowing			•		•	•	•									
A Walk in the Rain					•	•		•								
Exploration						•	•					•				
Lost Land	•					•						•				

Cross Reference of Major Topics

	Progressive Muscle Relax.	Breathing	Self-Esteem	Creativity	Testing	Academics	Imagination	Seasons/Nature	Positive Thinking	Senses	Growing/Changing	Motivation	Sharing	Peer Pressure	Acceptance	Health
Inspiration	•			•		•						•				
Listen	•					•		•		•						
Finding Treasure	•					•	•					•				
Book Adventure						•	•					•				
APPRECIATE																
(pp. 128–148)																
Good News			•						•		•					
Pillar of Strength							•		•				•			
Pumpkin Patch								•		•					•	
Attic Visit			•								•				•	
Get Away			•				•									
One of a Kind			•											•		
Self Sculpture			•				•	•			•				•	
Mysterious Music							•				•				•	
Endless Stream								•					•			
Around the World										•			•		•	
Surprise Season								•			•				•	
Drawer of Memories			•						•							
X-PAND																
(pp. 152–172)																
Pleasant Dreams	•		•				•		•							•
Fish Story								•		•						•
Going Places		•						•								•
Hidden Beauty								•	•							
Smoke Signals								•								•
Happy Landings								•								
Something/Nothing				•				•								
Winning Attitude									•							
Paint a Picture			•											•		•
Time Travel			•				•				•					
Dream On	•															•

Release
R
E
L
A
X

*"That serene and blessed mood. . . .
with an eye made quiet by the power of harmony, and the deep power of joy, we see into the life of things."*
—Wordsworth's
"The Abbey"

Learning progressive muscle relaxation and breathing exercises.

PMR 1

Relaxing Arms and Hands

Objective

Students will learn to relax their hands and arms by tensing and relaxing their muscles. Attention will be focused on their awareness of the contrasting feelings of tension and relaxation.

Script

Sit comfortably with your feet on the floor and your eyes closed. Take three long, deep breaths. (pause) Feel yourself relaxing more and more with each breath. Let the rhythm of the music calm you. Feel your muscles relax and your heart and breathing slow. Say to yourself, "I am calm and relaxed."

Listen to my voice and try your very best to do exactly as I say. As you listen to my voice let all other noises fade away. Listening, breathing slowly, feeling more and more relaxed.

Now pretend you have a warm lump of clay in your right hand. Squeeze it as hard as you can. Make your right hand into a tight fist. Squeeze it closed as hard as you can. Now hold it closed while I count to four; one, two, three, four. Now relax your right hand and let it go limp. Feel the difference. Feel how good it is to have a relaxed hand. Now squeeze it closed once more. Feel the warm clay ooze through your fingers as you tighten your right hand. Right fist clenched. Hold it tightly shut. Feel the tension. Good job! Now relax your right hand. Smooth out the tension and feel the relaxation. Right hand feeling heavy, relaxed and warm. You may even feel the air current surrounding your limp and relaxed right hand. Now keep your right hand relaxed while we concentrate on your left hand. (Repeat above script substituting left for right).

Good job! Now relax your whole body while you take a deep breath. Let the air out slowly, and say the words **"calm" and "relax"**. Be aware of this feeling of relaxation. Imagine yourself relaxing your hands tonight while you lay in bed. Imagine tightening the muscles in your hands and then relaxing those muscles. Relaxing at night can help you fall asleep.

Now, bend your right arm at the elbow and tighten all the muscles in your right arm. Make a muscle in your right arm and squeeze it hard. Hold the tension now while I count to four; one, two, three, four. Good job! Relax your arm now and let it go limp. Limp and relaxed. Heavy, relaxed, hands warming. Feel the good feeling of relaxation. Relax your arm completely. Say the words, "calm" and "relax" to yourself. Now tense the muscles in your right arm by making another muscle. Bend your arm at the elbow and bring your fist to your right shoulder. Squeeze hard. Hold the tension. Good job! Now relax your whole body while you take a deep breath. Let the air out slowly. Say the words "calm" and "relax". Be aware of this feeling of relaxation. Imagine yourself relaxing your hands tonight while you lay in bed. Imagine tightening the muscles in your hands and then relaxing those muscles. Feel the tension, feel the tightness. Now relax your right arm, let your arm drop to your side. Let go of all the tension in your right arm and hand. As you relax your right arm and hand you may feel it get heavier and heavier. Hands warming. Relaxation is the opposite of tension . You can relax by taking a deep breath, saying the words, "calm" and "relax", and letting go of all the tension in your muscles. Now keep your right arm and hand relaxed while you relax your left arm and hand. (Repeat above script substituting left for right.) Take a few moments to appreciate the good feeling of relaxation. Now as you do so, slowly allow yourself to come back to the room. Open your eyes. Stretch your arms and mind.

I would like you to practice relaxing your hands and arms tonight when you go to bed. Tell a parent what you have learned today. Remember to squeeze a pretend lump of clay so hard that it oozes between your fingers.

Discussion

How did it feel when you tensed your muscles? What part was hard to do? Could you feel the difference between feeling tense and feeling relaxed?

PMR 2

Relaxing Legs and Feet

Objective

Students will learn to relax their legs and feet by tensing and relaxing their muscles.

Script

Sit comfortably with your feet on the floor and your eyes closed. Take three long, deep breaths. (pause) Feel yourself relaxing more and more with each breath. Let the rhythm of the music calm you. Feel your muscles relax and your heart and breathing slow. Say to yourself, "I am calm and relaxed."

Take another deep breath. Listen to my voice and try your very best to do exactly what I say. Pretend that there is a rope that runs from your toes on your right foot to your right knee. Pull on that rope so your toes point toward your knee. Pull hard so you feel tension in your right leg, ankle and foot. Now relax your right leg. (Repeat for left leg.)

Pull both ropes now so both sets of toes are pointing to your knees. Tense all the muscles in your legs and ankles. Feel the tension. Now relax your legs and feel the difference. Feel how good it is to relax your legs. Relax your ankles, feet and toes. Relaxation is the opposite of tension. Now push your feet down. Pretend you are stepping into sand and want to bury your feet. Push them down hard and feel the tension in your legs, ankles and feet.

Hold that tension while I count to four; one, two, three, four. Good, now relax your legs, relax your feet, relax your toes. Let all your muscles go limp and soft. Feel all the tension drain from your body.

Now slowly come back to your room. Open your eyes and stretch. (pause) Listen to your teacher. Practice relaxing your legs and feet tonight at home.

Discussion

Did you feel the difference between feeling tense and relaxed? What part of your body seemed to relax the fastest? When is a good time for you to practice relaxing?

PMR 3

Relaxing Shoulders, Neck and Face

Objective

Students will learn to relax their shoulders, neck and face by tensing and relaxing their muscles.

Script

Sit comfortably with your feet on the floor and your eyes closed. Take three long, deep breaths. (pause) Feel yourself relaxing more and more with each breath. Let the rhythm of the music calm you. Feel your muscles relax and your heart and breathing slow. Say to yourself, "I am calm and relaxed."

Take another deep breath. As you let the air out relax your whole body. Tense your shoulders and neck by pulling your shoulders up to your ears. Hold your shoulders in that position. Feel the tension in your back, shoulders and neck. Hold that tension as I count to four; one, two, three, four. Now let your shoulders drop. Feel the relaxation as you rest your shoulders. Neck relaxed. Shoulders relaxed. Now raise your shoulders up once more. Pull them up right to your ears. Feel the tension in your neck, shoulders, and back. Now drop your shoulders. Relax your neck, shoulders and back. Now, pull your shoulders up one more time. Feel the tension. Hold it while I count to four; one, two, three, four. Relax your shoulders. Feel your upper back, shoulders and neck relaxing. Now close your eyes as tight as you can. Squeeze them shut. Feel your face muscles tighten even more by biting down hard. Hold the tension . . . squeeze hard. Now relax your face. Keep your eyes closed but not squeezed shut. Relax your jaw. Feel the difference. Take a deep breath and relax your whole body.

Once again squeeze your eyes closed. Pretend there are lead weights attached to the end of your eyelids pulling them down even farther. Bite down as hard as you can. Feel the tension on your face. Now relax your face. Feel the tension fade away. Now wrinkle your forehead muscles. Scrunch them up and hold the tension while I count to four; one, two, three, four. Now smooth out your forehead muscles. Smooth and relax. Let go of any tension in your face.

As your face relaxes feel the relaxation spread throughout your body. Take a deep breath and as you let it out allow yourself to slowly return to your room. Open your eyes and stretch. Be sure to practice relaxing your face, shoulders and neck tonight when you lay down in bed.

Discussion

Which muscles were the most difficult to relax? What feelings do you get when you take a deep breath?

PMR 4

Relaxing Lower Body

Objective

Students will practice relaxing their lower body by tensing and releasing their muscles. Attention will be focused on their awareness on the contrasting feelings of tension and relaxation.

Script

Sit comfortably with your feet on the floor and your eyes closed. Take three long, deep breaths. (pause) Feel yourself relaxing more and more with each breath. Let the rhythm of the music calm you. Feel your muscles relax and your heart and breathing slow. Say to yourself, "I am calm and relaxed."

Take another deep breath. Think about your toes. Now scrunch them up in your shoes as tight as you can and keep them tight. Now straighten your legs and tense all the muscles in your upper and lower leg by trying to pull your toes toward your knees. Hold this tension while I count to four; one, two, three, four. Good, now relax your toes, feet, ankles and legs. Put your feet flat on the ground and feel your legs get heavier and heavier. Relaxation is the opposite of tension. Relax your toes, ankles and legs. Toes relaxed, ankles relaxed, legs feeling heavier and heavier.

Now take another deep breath and hold it. Feel the tension (pause). Now release it and breathe slowly and easily. With each breath becoming more and more relaxed. Think of being so relaxed that you feel yourself floating down through your chair. Floating yet heavy. Relaxed muscles, clear mind, slow breathing. Now tense the muscles in your hips and stomach. Make your stomach muscles hard. Hold this tense feeling while I count to four; one, two, three, four. Release the tightness and relax the muscles in your hips and stomach. Stomach relaxed, hips relaxed, legs and feet relaxed, breathing slowing.

Now tense your stomach once more. Make the muscles hard and tense. Hold the tension. Stomach tense and hard...good. Now release the tension. Smooth muscles, relaxed stomach, relaxed hips. Legs and feet relaxed. Toes floating. Breathing slowing. Relaxation is the opposite of tension.

Take a moment to appreciate the good feelings of relaxation. Say to yourself, "I am calm and relaxed." Lower body relaxed and heavy. With each breath, more relaxation. Listen to the music and let any tension float down through your body and out your toes. Now as you do this slowly, allow yourself to come back to the room. Open your eyes and stretch (pause). I would like you to practice relaxing your lower body tonight when you are laying in bed. Remember to relax your toes, feet, legs, hips and stomach.

Discussion.

How did it feel when you became relaxed? When else could you practice these exercises? Why is it good to relax your body?

PMR 5

Relaxing Upper Body

Objectives

Students will practice relaxing their upper body parts by tensing and relaxing their muscles. Attention will be focused on their awareness of the contrasting feelings of tension and relaxation.

Script

Sit comfortably with your feet on the floor and your eyes closed. Take three long, deep breaths. (pause) Feel yourself relaxing more and more with each breath. Let the rhythm of the music calm you. Feel your muscles relax and your heart and breathing slow. Say to yourself, "I am calm and relaxed."

Take another deep breath. As you breathe out feel all the tension drain from your lower body. Relax your toes, feet and ankles.

Release all the tension from your legs. Feet relaxed, legs relaxed. With each breath deeper and deeper relaxation. You may begin to notice your legs getting heavier and heavier. With each breath, heart rate slows and relaxation spreads.

Now tense your stomach muscles, make them tight and hard. Hold that tension while I count to four; one, two, three, four. Good, now relax your stomach, smooth out the muscles. Feel your stomach relaxing more and more.

Now make a fist with your right hand. Pretend you are superman, squeezing a piece of coal so hard it turns into a diamond. Feel the tension in your right fist and arm as you continue to squeeze. Now relax your hand, release the tension. Let your hand and arm relax. Now squeeze your left fist together, tense all the muscles in your arm, shoulder and fist. Squeezing and tensing all the muscles of your left hand and arm. Hold the tension. Now release the tension and feel the muscles relax. Relaxing both arms, both hands. Fingers relaxed. Arms beginning to feel heavier and heavier. You may even notice a tingling feeling in your fingers as your hands warm. Arms relaxed and heavy. Lower body and stomach relaxed. Chest relaxed. Now as you relax your arms, pull your shoulders up toward your ears and hold them while I count to four... shoulders up, tension in your back and neck...one, two, three, four. Drop your shoulders. Relax your neck. Arms and hands relaxed. Breathing slow and easy.

As you exhale the tension flows out of your body. Body relaxed, arms feeling heavy and relaxed, hands warming. Legs and feet relaxed.

Now tense the muscles in your scalp and forehead by raising your eyebrows as high as you can. Feel the tension in your forehead. Hold it. Now relax your forehead and scalp. Smooth out all the muscles in your face. Eyes relaxed and closed; face relaxed; jaw relaxed.

Now take a deep breath and as you breath out feel your body become even more relaxed and let yourself slowly come back to the room. Open your eyes and stretch (pause).

Be sure to practice relaxing your upper body at home tonight. A good time to do this is when you are laying in bed getting ready to fall asleep.

Discussion

Is it getting easier to relax? Which muscles relaxed the best? When is another time you could practice these exercises?

PMR 6

Relaxing the Whole Body

Objective

Students will learn to relax their whole body by using the phrase "calm and relax", deep breathing and muscle relaxation.

Script

Sit comfortably with your feet on the floor and your eyes closed. Take three long, deep breaths. (pause) Feel yourself relaxing more and more with each breath. Let the rhythm of the music calm you. Feel your muscles relax and your heart and breathing slow. Say to yourself, "I am calm and relaxed."

Take another deep breath and as you let it out release all the tension from your whole body. Relax your forehead and facial muscles. Feel the muscles in your neck and shoulders and tell them to relax. As you continue to relax notice your breathing slowing down. Feel the muscles in your hands and arms and tell them to relax. Let go of all the tension in your face, neck, shoulders, arms and hands. Say to yourself, calm and relax and feel your whole body become even more relaxed. Chest and stomach muscles relaxed. Tell your legs and feet to relax. As you continue to relax say the words, "calm" and "relax" to yourself over and over. Calm and relax. You can use these words anytime you feel nervous and tense and your body will respond by becoming relaxed.

Now feel yourself drifting further and further into deep relaxation. You may notice a heavy feeling in your arms and legs. Each breath helps you relax even more. Enjoy the feeling of relaxation. Practice relaxing when you feel tense or nervous.

Now take a deep breath and as you let it out allow yourself to slowly come back to your room. Open your eyes and stretch (pause). Practice relaxing your whole body tonight at home. Tell a parent or a friend what you have learned and show them how to relax.

Discussion

How did that feel? Was it hard or easy to relax your whole body? Would it help you to relax yourself before a test?

PMR 7

Quick Relaxation Exercise

Objective

Students will learn a brief, relaxation exercise that can be used in a variety of settings.

Script

Sit comfortably with your feet on the floor and your eyes closed. Take three long, deep breaths. Feel yourself relaxing more and more with each breath. Let the rhythm of the music calm you. Feel your muscles relax and your heart and breathing slow. Say to yourself , "I am calm and relaxed."

Today we will learn a very brief or short way to achieve relaxation. Listen very carefully and do exactly what I say. First, get into a comfortable position. Second, take a deep breath, hold it and as you are holding your breath look up with your eyes. Keep your head still. Try to look at your eyebrows. Now close your eyes and let your eyes relax. Slowly breath out and say to yourself the words, "calm" and "relax". Let go of any tension in your body and allow your whole body to become fully relaxed. Be aware of your body and tell any part that is not relaxed to relax completely. Now take another deep breath and as you let it out tell your body to relax even more. Take another deep breath and as you let it out allow yourself to come back to your room. Open your eyes and stretch (pause).

Practice this exercise anytime you feel nervous or tense. Remember, just take a deep breath and hold it. Look up to your eyebrows without moving your head. Close your eyes and slowly breathe out while relaxing your eyes and your whole body.

Use this brief relaxation exercise whenever you feel tense or anxious. Practice this exercise at home.

Discussion

Were you able to achieve a feeling of relaxation? When could you use this exercise?

Body Breathing

Objective

Children will experience relaxation through breathing and active imagination.

Script

Sit comfortably with your feet on the floor and your eyes closed. Take three long, deep breaths. (pause) Feel yourself relaxing more and more with each breath. Let the rhythm of the music calm you. Feel your muscles relax and your heart and breathing slow. Say to yourself, "I am calm and relaxed."

As you become more relaxed, your breathing will be slow and even. Focus on your feet as they remain anchored to the floor. As you continue to breathe deeply, feel warm air come through the floor and open up a hole in your shoes. Feel the warm, fresh air pass your ankles and slowly rise up into your lower legs.

As the air expands in your knees, you are feeling calm and relaxed. Breathe in, and feel the air warm your thighs and surround your hips. Feel the air moving up through your stomach and into your chest. The warmth of your chest as it expands, relaxes you. Breathe deeply, and feel the air soothe your arms and fingers. Now, the muscles of your neck soak up the warm air. Feel your neck relax, barely able to support your head. Your body is now full.

You are calm and relaxed. Now breathing slowly repeat to yourself three times the following thought: "**My breathing is slow and deep....**" (pause) Breathe slowly next time you feel nervous or tense.

Take a deep breath and return to your room. Open your eyes and stretch. (pause) Take a few moments to appreciate the good feelings that come with relaxation.

My breathing is slow and deep.

Discussion

Did your breathing slow down? Do you feel more relaxed when you breath slowly? What happens to your breathing when you are upset, scared, or worried?

Activities

• Imagine you are in a beautiful garden and slowly breathe in all of the fresh scented air. Think of your favorite smell and breathe it in slowly.

• Think of a time or place where you become tense or nervous. Next time this happens take three deep breaths.

Push and Relax

Objective

To give children an activity they can use anytime of the day to relax and focus their attention.

Script

Releasing tension relaxes me.

Sit comfortably with your feet on the floor and your eyes closed. Take three long, deep breaths. (pause) Feel yourself relaxing more and more with each breath. Let the rhythm of the music calm you. Feel your muscles relax and your heart and breathing slow. Say to yourself, "I am calm and relaxed."

Take a slow, even breath and put your feet flat on the floor directly below you. Push your feet down. Feel your ankles, calves and upper legs become tense. Relax your feet. Feel calmness return to your legs. Take a deep breath and again push your feet against the floor. As you continue to push harder, feel tension in your ankles, calves, upper legs, stomach, chest and neck muscles. Now relax and feel comfort return to your entire body.

Take a breath and push your feet as hard as you can against the floor. Feel your entire body tense up. Hold it. Hold it, until I say relax. When I tell you to let go, feel the strength and steadiness of the floor fill your entire body. Relax. Breathe in and feel the added strength in your body. Say to yourself three times, **"Releasing tension relaxes me. . ."**(pause) Use this feeling of strength for the rest of the day. If you need extra strength, use this exercise at any time to recharge your batteries.

Take a deep breath and return to you room. Open your eyes and stretch. (pause) Take a few moments to appreciate the good feelings that come with relaxation.

Discussion

What are some situations where using this exercise might help you relax?

Activities

• The next time you are tense while at your desk or a table, sneak in a "push and relax" exercise. You can also do this exercise with your palms and forearms. You will find yourself relaxing and no one will know except the most important person— you!

• Read the following poem and invite students to participate.

Hands and Toes Relax

Pull your hands in a very tight fist
Now let them go up to your wrist.
Tight, tight, tight with all your might
Now just relax and make them light.

Curl your toes into a ball
Now let them go, release them all
Tight, tight, tight with all your might
Now just relax and make them light.

• Play "Adagio" (Dvorak) or suitable musical selection and ask children to tense and relax their bodies to the movements of the song. Variation: Move about the room in a dance of tension/relaxation.

•Using crayons and paper react to a classical song by "scribbling" to the music. Encourage children to use many strokes and colors. Name and sign your work of art and display it.

Breathe In, Breathe Out

Objective

The value of controlled, slow breathing accompanied by calming positive messages is introduced to the child.

Script

Sit comfortably with your feet on the floor and your eyes closed. Take three long, deep breaths. (pause) Feel yourself relaxing more and more with each breath. Let the rhythm of the music calm you. Feel your muscles relax and your heart and breathing slow. Say to yourself, "I am calm and relaxed."

Breathe slowly and deeply, in—out—in—out—
Breathe in relaxation, breathe out tension,
Breathe in calmness, breathe out all of your worries,
Breathe in warm sunshine, breathe out stale air.

I am special   Continue to breathe this way until you are calm and relaxed. Say to yourself, "I am calm and relaxed". Now give yourself positive messages as you breathe deeply, in—(pause) and out.

As you breathe in, say in your mind, **"I am . . ."** As you breathe out, say in your mind ". . . relaxed." Continue to breathe gently and deeply. Breathe in and say, "I am . . . " breathe out and say **special."** Think of a special talent you have or would like to have. (pause) Breathe in and say, "I am . . . breathe out and say your talent", "I am . . . (state your talent)", "I am . . . (state your talent)." Enjoy how you feel at this moment. Say these positive messages to yourself when you feel upset or worried.

Take a deep breath and return to your room. Open your eyes and stretch. (pause) Take a few moments to appreciate the good feelings that come with relaxation.

Discussion

What happened when you said "I am relaxed", "I am calm", "I am special"? What are some of your special talents?

Activities

•Take "breathing breaks" throughout the day. Breathe in deeply three times for extra energy or to relieve anxiety or stress.
•Create a cover for your journal. Record your talents or special abilities you would like to have. Set aside some time on a regular basis for journal writing. (Sample journal form in Appendix.)

Letting Go

Objective

The child will be introduced to full-body relaxation using the combination of muscle tension, relaxation and active imagination.

I am calm and relaxed.

Script

Sit comfortably with your feet on the floor and your eyes closed. Take three long, deep breaths. (pause) Feel yourself relaxing more and more with each breath. Let the rhythm of the music calm you. Feel your muscles relax and your heart and breathing slow. Say to yourself, "I am calm and relaxed."

Feel your toes, legs, stomach, shoulders, fingers, neck, jaw and face become as tight as a long rubber band that is stretched from one end of your desk (table, bed) to the other. Take a deep breath, and say the word "relax". As you exhale feel all of your tension disappear as your muscles relax. (pause) Say to yourself, **"I am calm and relaxed"**. . . (pause) Now breathe in and tense your whole body again. Hold this feeling for a few seconds. Say "relax" and breathe out the tightness in your body. (pause)

Say "relax" and feel your body loosen and become calm. (pause) Breathe in and tense your whole body like a tight ball of string. Feel your stomach, shoulders and neck tie themselves into knots. (pause) Now say "relax" and as you exhale feel the knots loosen and the string begins to unwind. As your string gets longer, you are more and more relaxed. Tie a kite onto your string. Climb the string and ride your kite as it floats through the clouds. Remember, you can carry the magic words "calm and relax" wherever you go.

Take a deep breath and return to your room. Open your eyes and stretch. (pause) Take a few moments to appreciate the good feelings that come with relaxation.

Discussion

Could you visualize yourself as a tight ball of string? Did you see yourself climb up the string? What other images did you have?

Activity

• While counting to ten have children progressively tighten up their entire body. When you say "let go", let them turn into rag dolls or jelly. Children can be challenged to tighten obscure muscles, e.g. eyelids, chin, eyebrows, etc.

Rainbow Walking

Objectives

Children are given the opportunity to practice seeing colors and introduced to the concept of a "special place" where they can return to be relaxed.

My mind is open and free.

Script

Sit comfortably with your feet on the floor and your eyes closed. Take three long, deep breaths. (pause) Feel yourself relaxing more and more with each breath. Let the rhythm of the music calm you. Feel your muscles relax and your heart and breathing slow. Say to yourself, "I am calm and relaxed."

Picture yourself standing on a rainbow high in the sky. A cool mist surrounds you. See the color red beneath your feet. In your mind say red then picture a delicious apple. Taste this apple. As you step down to the next ribbon of the rainbow think orange. Picture a bright orange sunset filling the sky. As you step down think yellow. Breathe in the warm yellow light. You are relaxing as you flow down the rainbow. Continue to walk down the rainbow and step to green, feel cool green grass tickle between your toes.

Your next step is blue. Think blue. Listen as cool blue water gurgles all around you. As you take your next step think violet, see rich violet colored flowers growing all around you. You are completely relaxed. All is calm. Now step off the rainbow and into your favorite place.

Think of your favorite place and see it in your mind. It is quiet and peaceful. You are warm and comfortable. Picture this place in your mind and say to your self three times, **"My mind is open and free.". . .** (pause) You can return to this peaceful place whenever you want.

Take a deep breath and return to your room. Open your eyes and stretch. (pause) Take a few moments to appreciate the good feelings that come with relaxation.

Discussion

Describe some characteristics of your special place. Which color of the rainbow is your favorite? What colors help you relax? Colors can affect how we feel. What is a red feeling? Explore other colors this way.

Activities

• Use watercolors or chalk to draw a rainbow.
• Talk about where you were the last time you saw a rainbow.
• Use a prism to look for the colors of the rainbow.

Wash Away Tension

Objectives

The child will experience full-body relaxation through the imagery of waves washing over his/her body parts.

I feel peaceful.

Script

Sit comfortably with your feet on the floor and your eyes closed. Take three long, deep breaths. (pause) Feel yourself relaxing more and more with each breath. Let the rhythm of the music calm you. Feel your muscles relax and your heart and breathing slow. Say to yourself, "I am calm and relaxed."

Imagine that you are sitting on the beach on a warm day. The sand is warm beneath you. Hear the sea birds above. The sound of the waves makes you calm and relaxed. The sun warms you from your toes to your head. Take a deep breath, and feel a wave come and wash over your feet. Breathe in as a wave approaches. Feel more relaxed as it washes over your knees. Breathe in and feel the water surround your upper legs and hips. Your lower body is relaxed. Breathe in, and feel the next wave smooth and relax your stomach. Breathe in, catch a wave and rub it on your chest, shoulders and arms. Feel them relax. Breathe in, and splash some water on your neck and face, releasing all tension.

Now breathe in and enjoy the warm feeling of your body completely relaxed. You feel relaxed as you experience the sand and the waves. Please repeat to yourself three times

"I feel peaceful". . . (pause) Remember your visit to the beach and your peaceful feeling.

Take a deep breath and return to your room. Open your eyes and stretch. (pause) Take a few moments to appreciate the good feelings that come with relaxation.

Discussion

Why is it relaxing to be at the seashore, the beach, a pool or in the water? Where are your favorite places to relax?

Activities

• Make a tape of the different water sounds in your home/school. Play the tape for others to try to figure out the sources of the sound.

• Listen to a commercially prepared tape of the ocean. Imagine you are there.

• Act out surfing on the waves, swimming in the oceans, etc.

Stairway To Relaxation

Objectives

I use my senses to relax.

The children will be given another opportunity to return to their special place. Visual images and sense of smell are used to enhance the feelings of relaxation.

Script

Sit comfortably with your feet on the floor and your eyes closed. Take three long, deep breaths. (pause) Feel yourself relaxing more and more with each breath. Let the rhythm of the music calm you. Feel your muscles relax and your heart and breathing slow. Say to yourself, "I am calm and relaxed."

Everything around you is calm, and you are relaxing. Breathe in and out slowly, evenly, throughout our travels today. Imagine yourself at the top of a long winding staircase. You enjoy the view, but want to step down into complete relaxation. Take a deep breath in. As you breathe out take one step down. Take a shallower breath in. As you release it move to the next step feeling even more calmness and relaxation. Breathe in then out and release yourself down to the next step. Breathe in then out and release yourself down to the next step. Continue to do this until you are at the bottom, totally relaxed.

You are in a quiet place, your special place. In your imagination you look around and see every color in the rainbow. Flowers are growing everywhere. Your favorite smell fills the air.

Breathe in and out your favorite smell. (pause) Now say to yourself three times, **"I use my senses to relax"**... (pause) Remain where you are and enjoy the feeling of relaxation.

Take a deep breath and let it out as you return to your room. Open your eyes and stretch. (pause) Take a few moments to appreciate the good feelings that come with relaxation.

Discussion

What feeling did you have as you walked down the stairs? What is your favorite smell? What kinds of feelings do you get when you sense that smell? Why do favorite smells help us relax and remember special times?

Activities

- Bake something special: cookies, popcorn, bread.
- Play a scent game by blindfolding each other and smelling different things. Identify the feeling evoked by the scents.
- Write a sentence for each of the senses. Example: The aroma of the cookies baking makes my mouth water.
- Read the following poem and try to imagine the smells:

I like the smell of strawberry pie,
and roses in the Spring.
The scent of a vanilla candle,
and thanksgiving turkey wing.
I like the smell of new-mown grass,
and raked up leaves in Fall.
I like to sniff mom's spice-shelf,
and a brand new basketball.

- Have a variety of scented soaps on a tray. Let the children smell them. "Paint" a picture by rubbing the bars of soap on black paper.

Books to Share

Aliki. *My Five Senses*
Durbor, C. *Where Is Your Nose?*

Cloud Of Calmness

Objectives

Children continue to practice relaxation techniques. Key words are calm, letting go, open, unique and dream. The child is asked to identify something they are good at.

Script

I can let go and relax.

Sit comfortably with your feet on the floor and your eyes closed. Take three long, deep breaths. (pause) Feel yourself relaxing more and more with each breath. Let the rhythm of the music calm you. Feel your muscles relax and your heart and breathing slow. Say to yourself, "I am calm and relaxed."

In your imagination, look up at the sky. See the word CLOUD floating peacefully before your eyes. Focus on the letter C. C stands for *calm*. Breathe in the fresh air of calmness. Let the air go and relax. Look at the letter L. L stands for *letting go*. Breathe in deeply. Breath out and let go of all the tight muscles in your body. See in your mind the letter O. Breathe in the O and use it to *open* your mind to new thoughts and ideas. Let go of the breath but keep your mind open. Continue to look at the sky and now see the letter U. U is for you and your *uniqueness*. Breathe in and think of something you are good at or would like to be good at as you breath out. Take one more deep breath and repeat one positive thought about yourself. (Pause) Let any tension or bad thoughts go when you exhale. (Pause) The last letter is D. D means *dream*. Dream about a special place.

Breathe quietly and dream of yourself floating on a fluffy cloud. Feel the sun warming and illuminating you. Drift with the breeze. Become any shape you want to. Feel totally relaxed. Now say to yourself three times, **"I let go and relax"**. . . (pause) You feel refreshed and light as a summer breeze.

Take a deep breath and return to your room. Open your eyes and stretch. (pause) Take a few moments to appreciate the good feelings that come with relaxation.

Discussion

What did you choose as something you are good at doing? What shape cloud did you become? Why is it helpful to think positive thoughts?

Activities

• Go outside (or look through a window) at the clouds and look for shapes. Make up a story about what you see. As the breeze changes the clouds, think of how you can change tense feelings into relaxed feelings.

• Color a picture. Use cotton balls for clouds. Put your picture on a wall where you can see it each day. As you look at it, recall your refreshed, relaxed feelings.

• Make a cloud. Pour an inch of very hot water in a jar and quickly cover it with a pie pan filled with ice cubes. Darken the room then shine a flashlight in the jar to see a "cloud of calmness."

• Pretend a parachute/sheet is a cloud and the children are the wind. Wave the parachute/sheet slowly. Increase the speed, then slow down. The children can lightly fall to the ground as soft as a cloud.

• Read the following poem and invite children to participate:

Bend and stretch, reach for the sky.
Take a deep breath. You feel good inside.
Bend and stretch, reach for the sky.
Put your cares on clouds. Now wave them goodbye.

Books To Share

DePaola, Tomie. *The Cloud Book*
Renberg, Dalia Hardoff. *Hello Clouds*
Spiers, Peter. *Dreams*
Freeman, Don. *Dandelion*
Shaw, Charles. *It Looked Like Spilt Milk*

Solar Energy

Objectives

Children will experience total body relaxation by imagining a light replacing feelings of tension. A message suggesting creative energy is provided.

Script

I am filled with creative energy.

Sit comfortably with your feet on the floor and your eyes closed. Take three long, deep breaths. (pause) Feel yourself relaxing more and more with each breath. Let the rhythm of the music calm you. Feel your muscles relax and your heart and breathing slow. Say to yourself, "I am calm and relaxed."

Feel a warm ray of sunlight on the top of your head. The light slowly spreads through your head, down through your eyebrows and eyelids. As the light spreads, your muscles relax. The light is now flowing down to your nose and jaw. Your tongue and chin feel relaxed. The light moves downward, relaxing the muscles of your neck and then your shoulders. It spreads outward, through your shoulders, down your arms, to your fingertips. The light spreads down through your upper body, down into your stomach.

Feel the light move slowly into your hips. Relax the hip muscles. The light moves down through each leg, down the thigh, knee, ankle, toes. You are totally relaxed. You are calm. All the tension has been replaced by light. Any remaining tension now flows out the tips of your fingers and your toes.

Concentrate on the warm, glowing feeling you have throughout your body. You could light up a room. Take a deep breath, and say to yourself three times, **"I am filled with creative energy"**. . . (pause)

Take a deep breath and let it out as you return to your room. Open your eyes and stretch. (pause) Take a few moments to appreciate the good feelings that come with relaxation.

Discussion

Do relaxation and creativity go together? When do you have your most creative thoughts? Where do you have them?

Activities

• Find a sunny window to sit at and read. Choose a story that is enjoyable to read. Remember the warm, sunny feelings you have.

the shapes.

• Think of a cat curled up in the sun and curl your body like a cat and then stretch like a cat.

• Create a sunlight photograph. Place a dark sheet of construction paper in bright sunlight. Place objects such as leaves atop the paper. Remove the objects after one hour and look at the sunlight photograph.

• Make a sundial by inserting a small dowel or pencil in the middle of a paper plate. Mark the position of the shadow every hour. Use the sundial to tell time the following day.

• Draw a circle then put rays around it to make a sun. On each ray write a feeling you have when out in the sun. Put a happy face in the circle.

Books to Share

Gibbons, Gail. *Sun Up, Sun Down*
Peters, Lisa. *Sun, the Wind and the Rain*

Rolling Waves

Objective

Children will achieve a feeling of relaxation by progressively relaxing body parts.

Script

I am able to relax myself.

Sit comfortably with your feet on the floor and your eyes closed. Take three long, deep breaths. (pause) Feel yourself relaxing more and more with each breath. Let the rhythm of the music calm you. Feel your muscles relax and your heart and breathing slow. Say to yourself, "I am calm and relaxed."

Take a slow even breath. You are sitting on a sandy beach on a warm lazy summer day. Curl your toes and feel the moist sand ooze out. As you listen to the sound of the waves washing the shoreline you become more and more relaxed. Concentrate on the rhythm of the music, which like the waves, calms you. (pause)

Feel a wave come up and tickle your toes. As you watch the waves come in you notice that each one is different. Watch as a wave deposits a bit of seaweed on the shore. Watch as a wave covers a small shiny stone with sand. Watch as the next wave uncovers a beautiful pink and brown shell. Pick it up and put it to your ear. Listen carefully to the shell's echo of the waves. It whispers relax. . .relax. . .relax. . . Watch as a footprint slowly fills with water. Before long it disappears completely.

Make a hand print in the cool damp sand next to you. It too becomes flat again. Look at the waves themselves as they gently roll in. Each one reaches the shore with a different height and force. Watch as a small wave laps the shore. What sound does it make? Watch as a medium wave creeps up higher. What sound does it make? Watch as a large wave topped with white bubbles runs up the beach turning dry white sand a brown color. What sound does it make?

Listen to the music of the waves. (pause) Move down closer to the water. A small wave creeps in and washes away remaining tensions you may have in your feet. Now a medium wave comes up to relax your legs and seat. A large wave arises to soothe your chest and arms. You feel totally cleansed and refreshed. Concentrate on how good it feels to have the tension in your body replaced with calm peaceful feelings. Take a slow, even breath. Repeat to yourself three times, **"I am able to relax myself"**. . . (pause) Remember if you feel tense, breathe deeply and see and hear the rhythm of the waves. They are always there to help you relax.

Take a deep breath and return to your room. Open your eyes and stretch. (pause) Take a few moments to appreciate the good feelings that come with relaxation.

Discussion

This is our second visit to the beach. Why are sand and water used as images of relaxation? Why is it important to relax? Have you tried to use your ability to relax in other places or times in your life?

Activities

• Fill a pan with sand, salt or dry Jello. Make your hand prints in it. A lasting print can be made using plaster.

• Use an empty gallon ice cream bucket to make an underwater scene. Cut a large oval opening in one side of the container. Paint the inside and outside of the container blue. Cut out fish and seaweed shapes. Tape clear plastic wrap to the opening of the container. Glue in fish and seaweed. Fill the bottom of the container with sand. Add seashells to complete the aquarium.

• Take off your shoes and socks. Giggle and wiggle your toes. Curl your toes then relax them.

Books To Share

Goudey, Alice. *Houses From The Sea*
Lionni, Leo. *Swimming*

Color Connecting

Objectives

Children are given an opportunity to practice imagining colors. The visual image of a rainbow is used as a key image to connect the feelings of energy, creativity and relaxation.

Script

I am energetic.

Sit comfortably with your feet on the floor and your eyes closed. Take three long, deep breaths. (pause) Feel yourself relaxing more and more with each breath. Let the rhythm of the music calm you. Feel your muscles relax and your heart and breathing slow. Say to yourself, "I am calm and relaxed."

You see a beautiful rainbow. It is close and you can see both ends and all the colors. The top of the bow reaches into the heavens. The colors merge one into another. (Pause between colors to give students a chance to visualize them.) Red into orange. . . orange into yellow. . . yellow into green. . . green into blue. . . and finally blue into violet. As you look you feel calm and relaxed. The rainbow seems to be close; so close you can almost touch it. You reach out your hand towards the brilliant colors. It moves towards you. You can touch it!

Now you are standing under one end of the rainbow as it comes down from the heavens. The colors cover you from head to toe. There is an energy flowing through you. Your mind seems to be energized. Full of feelings and ideas. Say to yourself three times, **"I am energetic"**. . . (pause) Slowly the rainbow fades away. You remain calm and relaxed. Your mind remains open and creative.

Take a deep breath and return to your room. Open your eyes and stretch. (pause) Take a few moments to appreciate the good feelings that come with relaxation.

Discussion

Did you feel a sense of energy flowing through you? Do you ever have too much energy? How do you let it out?

Activities

• Think of things to try when you feel you have too much energy.

• Pretend you are running to catch a rainbow. Pretend you are jumping high to touch a rainbow.

• Repeat a motion as fast as you can and then the same motion as slowly as you can.

Big Balloon

Objective

Children learn the association of deep breathing and the release of tension or anxiety.

Script

Sit comfortably with your feet on the floor and your eyes closed. Take three long, deep breaths. (pause) Feel yourself relaxing more and more with each breath. Let the rhythm of the music calm you. Feel your muscles relax and your heart and breathing slow. Say to yourself, "I am calm and relaxed."

Get comfortable in your seat. Lean back just a little, then place one hand gently on your stomach. Breathe deeply and feel your hand move up and down . . . up and down.

Imagine a balloon inside your stomach. Now, breathe in deeply and slowly and blow up the balloon. (pause) As you breathe out, empty all of the air out of the balloon. (pause)

Blow up the balloon again with a deep, long breath. (pause) As you exhale, let the air escape quietly through your mouth. (pause)

Blow up the balloon again. (pause) This time exhale the air through your nose. (pause) Now breathe in deeply and blow up the balloon even bigger than before. (Read quickly) Now imagine your balloon is ready to pop. Keep your balloon big and when I say pop, let the air explode out of you. POP!

Let some air back in and notice a warm feeling of relaxation. Enjoy this calm and relaxed feeling. Imagine balloons of every color floating over a rainbow across the sky. Take a deep breath and say three times as you breathe out, **"I can breathe out tension"**. . . (pause) Take your balloon with you whenever you are angry, tense or nervous.

Take a deep breath and return to your room. Open your eyes and stretch. (pause) Take a few moments to appreciate the good feelings that come with relaxation.

I can breathe out tension.

Discussion

When your balloon popped, did the air come out of your nose or mouth? Why is it important to have a way to relax yourself in a time of stress or anger?

Activity

• Play musical balloons. Use as many balloons as there are children minus one. Play music as children bat balloons around. When the music stops each child catches and holds onto a balloon. One child gets to pop a balloon for the next round.

R Enjoy
E
L
A
X

"Think of the happiest
things. Then you'll feel like
you have wings."
—Walt Disney's Peter Pan

Practice what you have learned about
relaxation while enjoying these scripts.

Toy Store Trip

Objectives

To introduce a message of appreciation for having fun.

Script

I am never too old to play and be happy.

Sit comfortably with your feet on the floor and your eyes closed. Take three long, deep breaths. (pause) Feel yourself relaxing more and more with each breath. Let the rhythm of the music calm you. Feel your muscles relax and your heart and breathing slow. Say to yourself, "I am calm and relaxed."

Take another deep breath and find yourself in a toy store. Toys of every shape and color are stacked from floor to ceiling. Listen to the many sounds that fill the air. Hear the high-pitched sounds of bells ringing and buzzers buzzing. Hear the sounds of laughter from people of all ages as they talk and play. In a toy store, everyone is a child. This store is the biggest of its kind in the world.

Breathe slowly, and begin your tour. You come upon the most fascinating video game that you have ever seen . You reach out with both hands, take the controls, and begin to play. The graphics are fantastic, the colors amazing. You float over every obstacle. Nothing can stop you. Listen to the music, and picture yourself achieving a perfect score on a video game. (pause)

You now stop to look at a toy train. This train is exactly like a real one, only smaller. Hear the whistle blow and see the wheels turn. Smell the oil and smoke. Watching the train go round and round relaxes you. (pause) Now look on the shelf, and see your favorite toy. Take it down, and hold it in your hands. Imagine yourself playing with it. Remember this feeling. (pause)

Look in the corner, and see a huge area filled with hundreds of small colorful plastic balls. Jump into the balls and feel them surround you. You move like you are in slow motion. The plastic balls massage and relax you. Feel your legs relax, your waist relax, your chest relax. Your entire body is calm and relaxed. Enjoy this feeling of relaxation (pause) Breathe slowly, and say to yourself three times, **"I am never too old to play and be happy"**. . . (pause)

Take a deep breath and return to your room. Open your eyes and stretch. (pause) Take a few moments to appreciate the good feelings that come with relaxation.

Discussion

What was the favorite toy you chose to play with? What are some things you do for fun? Talk about a time you had fun without toys or games.

Activity

• Make a game board or card game. Play your game with a friend.

Books To Share

Freeman, D. *Corduroy*
Weber, B. *Ira Sleeps Over*
Williams, M. *The Velveteen Rabbit*
Zolotow, C. *William's Doll*

Fall Fireworks

Objective

To have children become relaxed and to develop an appreciation of the beauty of a fall day.

I enjoy nature's beauty.

Script

Sit comfortably with your feet on the floor and your eyes closed. Take three long, deep breaths. (pause) Feel yourself relaxing more and more with each breath. Let the rhythm of the music calm you. Feel your muscles relax and your heart and breathing slow. Say to yourself, "I am calm and relaxed."

Picture yourself riding in a car. You are relaxed as you cruise down a long, narrow country road. Your seat belt holds you to your seat, but your mind begins to wander around the beautiful countryside. You breathe in and smell the sweet scent of a distant apple orchard.

It is autumn, and the trees are exploding with color. As you look around, it is like fireworks in the daytime. The breeze makes the leaves appear to change shades and move in rhythm. Look out the side window, and see the different shades of yellow come alive on the hillside. As your breathing slows you notice that, out the other side window, a brilliant orange color pops up everywhere in view. Relax and look ahead to see a spectacular display of red bursting all around.

You are at peace as you drive into this awesome display of color. (pause) You forget where you are going, as you continue down this colorful highway. Take some time now to get lost in the sights and smells which have surrounded your car. (pause) Notice new and beautiful colors. Breathe in wonderful new smells. Breathe deeply and as you exhale, say to yourself three times, **"I enjoy nature's beauty "**. . . (pause) Remember, nature's fireworks are just outside your window.

Take a deep breath and return to your room. Open your eyes and stretch. (pause) Take a few moments to appreciate the good feelings that come with relaxation.

Discussion

Share a pleasant memory of a fall day. If you have not experienced a colorful autumn, what do you think it would be like? Imagine a world without color. What would it be like? What problems might there be?

Activities

• Sponge paint an autumn picture. Display the pictures and when you look at them say to yourself, "I enjoy nature's beauty."

• Go for a walk and collect fall leaves. If you would like to save the leaves you can make a place mat. Take two pieces of waxed paper. Place your leaves between the two pieces. Press lightly and quickly with a warm iron.

• Read the following poem and invite students to participate.

Whirl

Like a leaf or feather
In windy, cold weather,
We will whirl around, (move slowly)
Without a sound,
And all sit down together.

—Author Unknown

Books to Share

Gibbons, Gail. *The Seasons of Arnold's Apple Tree*
Maestro, Betsy. *Why Do Leaves Change Color?*

Popcorn Fun

Objective

To give children an opportunity to practice using their imagination.

Script

I enjoy using my imagination.

Sit comfortably with your feet on the floor and your eyes closed. Take three long, deep breaths. (pause) Feel yourself relaxing more and more with each breath. Let the rhythm of the music calm you. Feel your muscles relax and your heart and breathing slow. Say to yourself, "I am calm and relaxed."

Breathe slowly and picture yourself as a kernel of popcorn in a dark jar. It is quiet and you are calm and relaxed. You are proud to be a kernel of popcorn, but you would like to get out of the glass that confines you and be able to truly express yourself. Take a deep breath and as you exhale think about the fresh world outside. (pause) Suddenly it becomes very bright as a gigantic scoop lifts you up and drops you into a strange place. Warm air surrounds you and hurls you up and down along with many other kernels. Feel the warm ride on a blanket of hot air, up, down, all around. Up down, all around. Enjoy the feeling of weightlessness. Your undercoat slowly becomes hot. You can hear steam hissing and feel its tickle as it tries to escape your outer shell. Strange smells fill the air. The noise of the hot air popper begins to be meshed with small explosions of white. Pop . . . pop. . . pop, pop. . . . Breathe in deeply. Let out the air and burst high into the air. You are a beautiful piece of popcorn like no other. As you float through the air, enjoy your new shape, smell and the light feeling you have. (pause)

Breathe slowly and think of a special popcorn memory you may have. Think of a happy time at home, at school, at the movies, a ball game, a circus. (pause) Repeat to yourself three times, **"I enjoy using my imagination. . ."** (pause) Be ready for good things to pop up for you for the rest of the day.

Take a deep breath and return to your room. Open your eyes and stretch. (pause) Take a few moments to appreciate the good feelings that come with relaxation.

Discussion

What is your favorite type of popcorn? What were some of your special popcorn memories? Describe how you felt when you escaped from that small confining kernel.

Activities

• Teacher may modify the activity by passing out popcorn before or after the experience. Coffee filters can be used as individual bowls.

• Use your imagination to role play the experience of being a kernel of popcorn. You can use just your head, just your foot or your whole body. Feel the burst of energy and the feeling of floating. Use these feelings to help you relax.

• Spread glue on a piece of paper in the shape of your name. Glue popped corn to the paper.

Book To Share

DePaola, Tomie. *The Popcorn Book*

Poem to Read

I am a popcorn kernel,
On the electric range,
With oil to my ankles,
Waiting for the change.

Pop, pop, its started happening,
The noise has just begun.
Pop, pop, there it goes again.
It sounds like lots of fun.

Explosions to the left of me.
Explosions to the right.
I'm just about to blow my top,
I really think I might. BANG!

—Dick Wilmes

The Complete Meal

Objective

I enjoy being with others during special times.

To enhance the feeling of special times by imagining being with a special friend or family member.

Script

Sit comfortably with your feet on the floor and your eyes closed. Take three long, deep breaths. (pause) Feel yourself relaxing more and more with each breath. Let the rhythm of the music calm you. Feel your muscles relax and your heart and breathing slow. Say to yourself, "I am calm and relaxed."

Breathe slowly and picture yourself sitting at a large dinner table. The table is set with candles and fine china. Food of every description is spread out before you. The dining room windows are steamed up. Someone has been cooking all day. Take a deep breath and smell the roasted turkey or other food. Take another breath and smell the freshly baked bread. Smell your favorite aroma. (pause)

Something is missing. The food is all there but no one is sitting around the table to share it with you. Your empty feeling is not in your stomach but in your heart. A feast like this must be shared with others. Take a deep breath, and as you breathe out look across the table and picture a special friend or family member you would like at your table. (pause) Breathe slowly, look to your left and picture another friend or family member you would like to eat with. As you continue to breathe slowly, look to your right and picture anyone else you would like joining you for this special meal. (pause)

You now feel calm and relaxed. . .and ready to eat. Pile your plate high with food. Hear the chatter and laughter of your friends. This is a time to be thankful. All becomes quiet as you raise your water glass for a toast. . . Say to yourself three times, **"I enjoy being with others during special times"**. . . (pause) It is fun to share special times with others.

Take a deep breath and as you breathe out, return to your room. Open your eyes and stretch. (pause) Take a few moments to appreciate the good feelings that come with relaxation.

Discussion

Share a memory of a past feast. Who shared that time with you? What are some things that you could do to make these times special?

Activities

• Create a place mat. Use the place mat at a special meal with your classmates (family).

• Write a letter to thank someone who has done something special for you.

• Have the children form a circle. Holding on to one end, a ball of yearn can be thrown to various people. When someone catches the ball, they should say something nice about the person who threw it.

• Plan a simple meal. Write an invitation to someone special to share the meal with you.

Books To Share

Moncure, Jane. *I Never Say I'm Thankful But I Am*
McGovern, Ann. *Stone Soup*

A Little Adventure

Objective

To provide an opportunity for enjoyment through the use of imagination.

Script

I am happy being me.

Sit comfortably with your feet on the floor and your eyes closed. Take three long, deep breaths. (pause) Feel yourself relaxing more and more with each breath. Let the rhythm of the music calm you. Feel your muscles relax and your heart and breathing slow. Say to yourself, "I am calm and relaxed."

Breathe in and out and feel yourself get a little smaller. Breathe slowly and you can barely see over your desk. Breathe in and out and you are now about the size of a ruler. Breathe slowly and it would take a magnifying glass just to see you. You are not afraid because you know this is just a game. Look down from your chair. The floor looks as big as a parking lot. Slide down the leg of your chair. Luckily for you, you land on a piece of soft dust.

There is so much to explore. You decide that you need to get to a very high spot and look around. As you walk, the desk and chair legs in your classroom look like giant metal tree trunks. Hop on a friendly bug and take a smooth ride to the front of the classroom. You thank him by removing a sliver that was lodged in one of his legs. In front of you is a tall thick piece of wood that will make a perfect observation tower. Using the grain of the wood to grab onto, you begin to climb.

After a while you reach a large flat desk surface. Take a minute to sit down and relax. You see another long stick of wood. This surely must be the highest and best lookout point in the classroom. Climb the wood until you reach the soft spongy pink top. You can look out and see the whole classroom. All at once you begin to rock back and forth. Get down on all fours and hold on for dear life. Look down and see a giant hand and piece of paper below you. You realize that you are perched on top of the teacher's pencil. You notice that she is writing a letter to your parent saying that you have run away from school. Scream and holler that you are on the pencil eraser right in front of her nose. "Here I am! Here I am!" You are so small that she cannot hear you. It's getting harder and harder to hold on to the pencil. The teacher makes a cursive e then two 1's and you are whipped off the pencil and onto the stamp pad on her desk.

You are unhurt but covered with purple ink. The teacher is getting ready to use her stamp pad. Look up to see a huge happy face stamp coming down on you. You are starting to grow, but will there be enough time? Breathe in deeply and feel yourself become bigger. Breathe in again and continue to grow. Breathe in one last time and return to normal size. You are sitting on the teacher's desk with a purple happy face stamped on your forehead. Everyone is totally shocked as you begin to laugh. Your classmates begin to laugh with you. You can understand their reaction.

Breathe slowly and repeat to yourself three times, **"I am happy being me"**. . . (pause)

Take a deep breath and return to your room. Open your eyes and stretch. (pause) Take a few moments to appreciate the good feelings that come with relaxation.

Discussion

Did you participate in the entire adventure? Is it easy for you to make a picture in your mind? How far back can you remember in your own life?

Activity

• Close your eyes and make a picture in your mind. Picture yourself being little. Now make a picture in your mind where you are big. Freeze a favorite moment in this story and color a picture of it.

Books To Share

Heide, Florence Parry. *The Shrinking of Treehorn*
Joyce, William. *George Shrinks*

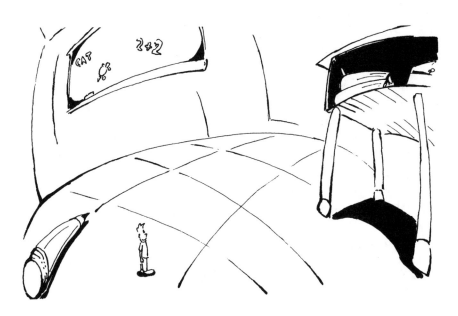

Airborne

Objective

To help children anticipate the future in a positive way.

I have much to see and enjoy in my life.

Script

Sit comfortably with your feet on the floor and your eyes closed. Take three long, deep breaths. (pause) Feel yourself relaxing more and more with each breath. Let the rhythm of the music calm you. Feel your muscles relax and your heart and breathing slow. Say to yourself, "I am calm and relaxed."

Take three slow breaths. Your chair becomes a comfortable bucket seat with arm rests and a head rest. A voice says, "Fasten your seat belt". Hear a loud whirling noise and feel your whole body being pushed back against your soft seat. Look out the small rectangular window next to you and see that the ground is just a blur because you are moving so fast. Your plane is about to take off. As the flaps on the wing go up your seat tilts back and you ascend quickly into the sky. Plug in your headphones attached to your seat and enjoy beautiful music and scenery.

Look down and see strange little objects moving like ants in an ant farm. As you look closer you discover these tiny things are cars following ribbons of roads in and out of the city. As you continue, the roads now seem to outline a giant checkerboard filled with shades of green and brown. The pilot tells you the squares are large fields filled with corn or wheat. Look down and see some bright blue puddles. You know that you must be looking at huge lakes. From the air, one lake looks a little like a turtle. Another one is in the shape of your favorite animal. Look closely until you see it. (pause)

The music and scenery helps you feel calm and relaxed. You now see a great mountain range. Some have caps of snow. You are up so high that even these majestic giants look small. Red canyons weave in and out of the mountain ranges. A blue-green river winds through them like a snake. You are above the birds. You are above the clouds. You feel like you're on top of the world. You imagine that if there was a storm you could just fly over it. Everything looks so neat and so clear.

On your cross country trip you have noticed a few cities and many beautiful wide open spaces. You realize that there are many wonderful places to go and things to do. You also know that you will find happiness somewhere below. Take a deep breath and repeat to yourself three times, **"I have much to see and enjoy in my life".** . . . (pause) You wish that you could jump on a cloud and stay in the air a while longer, but it is time for you to land. Pull your seat belt tight. If you feel that you're always climbing a mountain, return to your airplane for a much clearer picture. Somewhere out there is a place for you.

Take a deep breath and return to your room. Open your eyes and stretch. (pause) Take a few moments to appreciate the good feelings that come with relaxation.

Discussion

What are some of your dreams about your future? What would you like to do? Where would you like to live?

Activities

• Draw a map of your town the way it might look from an airplane.

• Choose a social studies curriculum area and take a "flight" together. Discuss the experience as it would appear from the sky. Design a postcard for the area and write a message to a family member or friend. Be sure to mention something that you are enjoying on your imaginary trip.

• Provide children with an assortment of materials such as styrofoam, wood, paint, glue, glitter, etc. Ask them to invent an imaginary airplane. Write a story about trips they took in their magic airplane.

Books To Share:

Calhoun, Mary. *Hot Air Henry*
Jeschke, Susan. *Perfect The Pig*

Candy Store

Objective

To create a set of positive responses for feeling capable of handling demanding tasks.

Script

No task is too large because I am full of energy.

Sit comfortably with your feet on the floor and your eyes closed. Take three long, deep breaths. (pause) Feel yourself relaxing more and more with each breath. Let the rhythm of the music calm you. Feel your muscles relax and your heart and breathing slow. Say to yourself, "I am calm and relaxed."

Breathe slowly and imagine that you are standing at the counter of a magnificent candy store. Look around and notice the many colors, shapes and sizes of the sweets. Today they are passing out free samples of hard peppermint candy. Pop a piece in your mouth and feel it tickle your taste buds and tease your nose.

Take a deep breath and smile as you look and see candy everywhere. Reach into your pocket, pull out your money and set it on the counter. You have chosen to buy the super duper, tutti-frutti sugarless gum. A man in a red and white striped shirt hands it to you. Quickly pop it into your mouth. Taste the gum as it fills your mouth with flavor. Feel calm and relaxed. (Pause) Put the gum on your tongue and begin to blow a bubble.

Take a deep breath in, then slowly blow out as a bubble begins to appear. Breath in. . .and blow out, making the bubble larger. Breathe in. . .and blow out again. The bubble becomes even larger. Repeat this breathing until the bubble becomes as big as YOU. This bubble gum must be magic! Step inside your big bubble and feel weightless, almost like an astronaut in space. Float around a little bit. You feel energized and free of tension as you bounce and float wherever you want. Up, up and away you go! As you slowly rise repeat to yourself three times, **"No task is too large because I am full of energy"**. . . (pause) Begin to float back now.

Take a deep breath and return to your room. Open your eyes and stretch. (pause) Take a few moments to appreciate the good feelings that come with relaxation.

Discussion

What are some things you can say to yourself when you feel something is too hard to do? Describe one time when you felt you really accomplished something. What is that feeling like?

Activities

• Chew a piece of bubble gum. Pretend you are being carried away by a big bubble. Write/talk about the trip. Where did you go? What did you see along the way? What did you do while you were traveling?

• Think about a difficult project that is coming up. When you are in the air, floating with your bubble, plan the things you will need to accomplish this task.

• Make a large pan of soapy water and blow bubbles. Observe the bubbles. Why do some bubles float along, following a path, while others burst? Try to catch a bubble.

Books to Share

Mayer, Mercer. *Bubble Bubble*
Durant, Penny Raife. *Bubblemania!*

Bouncing Ball

Objective

To give children hope of recovering from things that bother them.

**When I'm down
I can bounce back.**

Script

Sit comfortably with your feet on the floor and your eyes closed. Take three long, deep breaths. (pause) Feel yourself relaxing more and more with each breath. Let the rhythm of the music calm you. Feel your muscles relax and your heart and breathing slow. Say to yourself, "I am calm and relaxed."

See yourself standing on the deck of a large swimming pool. Breathe in and enjoy the clean smell of the chlorine in the water. Look through the crystal clear water and see all the way to the flat blue bottom of the pool. The little ripples of water on top make the lines on the bottom look like they are dancing for joy. Feel the sun reflect off the water and warm your entire body. Look down at your feet and see a brightly colored beach ball laying flat on the deck. Pick it up, take a big breath and begin to blow. It takes three large breaths to blow up the beachball. (pause)

Now look up at the lifeguard. She nods and says the water is not over your head. Jump in and make a big splash. You are surprised that the water is so warm. With your hand, make a big splash in every direction.

Take the beachball, hug it and push it under the water. It is hard to push down, but hold it at your waist. Let go and watch as the ball rushes to the top and pops out into the air. Grab the beachball and reload. This time, push the ball to your knees. Release it and watch as it goes even higher in the air. Now take it and struggle to push it all the way to the bottom of the pool. Let go and whoosh . . . the beach ball shoots through the air and almost out of sight. As you watch it float away repeat to yourself three times, **"When I'm down, I can bounce back"**. . . (pause) Take a breath and bounce out of the swimming pool. Dry yourself off.

Take a deep breath and return to your room. Open your eyes and stretch. (pause) Take a few moments to appreciate the good feelings that come with relaxation.

Discussion

There is a saying "what goes up, must come down." Our story today says "what goes down must come up." How does this relate to people's feelings?

Activities

• Provide children with bubble liquid and blower. Ask them to think of something that is bothering them. Have them blow that feeling into a bubble, then pop it.

• Stand in a circle. Play catch using a beach ball. When someone catches the ball they must say something nice about themselves. Do the same activity except this time they say something nice about the person next to them. Discuss how a positive thought or compliment can help someone bounce back from something that troubles them.

• Pretend your chest is a beach ball and fill it up with a deep breath. Let out the air through your lips making them vibrate and producing a funny sound. Ask the children to remember a time when laughter helped them bounce back when they were sad.

Books to Share

Moss, Marissa. *Regina's Big Mistake*
Payne, Lauren Murphy. *Just Because I Am*

Hidden Heroes

Objective

To increase the child's feeling of worth through active imagination.

Script

I feel good about who I am.

Sit comfortably with your feet on the floor and your eyes closed. Take three long, deep breaths. (pause) Feel yourself relaxing more and more with each breath. Let the rhythm of the music calm you. Feel your muscles relax and your heart and breathing slow. Say to yourself, "I am calm and relaxed."

Breathe slowly and notice that you are standing in front of a large door. You hear clapping and cheering on the other side. Take a deep breath, reach out, push, and slowly walk through the door. What a surprise! You walk into a magnificent indoor stadium. The seats are filled with people wearing your favorite team's color. Breathe in, and smell the hot dogs and freshly popped popcorn. Walk down the stadium stairs and onto the field. Your favorite sports star is standing right in front of you. Reach out and shake hands. You become friends and talk about many things. (pause) It is time to move on.

Picture yourself standing in front of a huge white mansion. It is a clear spring day. Take a deep breath, and smell the cherry blossoms which cover the trees in the yard. A long, black limousine with flags on the antennas, pulls up beside you. The tinted window comes down, and you see the President of the United States. The President motions for you to come over. You get in the car and begin to talk. As you drive around Washington D.C., you become friends. (pause) It is time to move on.

Find yourself backstage at a large theater. You are looking at a curtain with a bright star pinned to it. The curtain opens, and your favorite entertainer steps out and says "Hello". You quickly become friends. As the crowd cheers and the performance begins, you hear them dedicate the show to you. (pause) It is time to move on.

Breathe slowly. You are now sitting comfortably in the warmth of your own home. You feel calm and relaxed, happy and secure. Get up and walk into the next room. You see a table filled with your favorite food. There are balloons, streamers and presents everywhere. Your family and many friends have decided to give you a surprise party. They tell you that, even though you're not a star athlete, the President of the United States, or an entertainer, you are a famous person to them. You feel happy being just who you are. Repeat to yourself three times, **"I feel good about who I am"**. . . (pause) You decide that each morning when you get out of bed you'll say to yourself, "I'm OK, and I feel good about who I am."

Take a deep breath and return to your room. Open your eyes and stretch. (pause) Take a few moments to appreciate the good feelings that come with relaxation.

Discussion

Why is it sometimes harder to compliment ourselves than to compliment others? Why is it important to feel good about ourselves? How do we develop good feelings about ourselves.

Activities

• Look up the definition of the word "hero" in a dictionary. List qualities you think a hero should have.

• Help children realize their uniqueness by making "personality mirrors" Let each child cover a tagboard circle with aluminum foil.

Books To Share

Seeger, Pete. *Abiyoyo* (South African Folk Tale)
Seuss, Dr. *Happy Birthday to You*
Van Allsburg, Chris. *The Polar Express*
Waber, Bernard. *Lyle and the Birthday Party*

Bicycle Trip

Objective

To help children develop a visual link of feeling confident about themselves by being in control of a magic bicycle.

Script

I feel confident about who I am.

Sit comfortably with your feet on the floor and your eyes closed. Take three long, deep breaths. (pause) Feel yourself relaxing more and more with each breath. Let the rhythm of the music calm you. Feel your muscles relax and your heart and breathing slow. Say to yourself, "I am calm and relaxed."

Breathe in again, and smell the freshness of country air. You are riding your bike down a beautiful tree-lined road. You can see for miles in front of you. The wind is at your back, and you are headed down a long, gradual hill. Your seat becomes completely comfortable, and your feet become part of the pedals. You feel calm and relaxed. The more relaxed you feel, the easier it is to ride. Glide effortlessly, and let your mind wander. (pause)

Take a deep breath, and breathe out any tension you may have in your body. Feel your bicycle rise a few inches off the ground. Take another deep breath. Breathe out any hidden worry and enjoy the feeling as your bike floats a few feet into the air. Take a deep, deep breath and hold it. Search your body for any remaining tightness, and then exhale. As you breathe out this tension, you and your bicycle take off like a bird.

You can take your magic bicycle anywhere you want. You feel totally safe and free. Enjoy the clear air and the warm breeze against your face. The scenery below is magnificent. You are calm and relaxed. Pull up on your handlebars, and feel your bike go straight up. Pull up again, and do a loop, just as if you were on a floating Ferris wheel. Practice other turns and tricks, as you calmly control your bike. (pause)

Your magic machine can also skywrite. Write a message. (pause) Turn on any color you want, and write the following message for all to see down below. . ."I feel confident about who I am". . . (pause) Take a deep breath, and repeat to yourself three times the message you wrote in the sky, **"I feel confident about who I am. . . ."** (pause) Take a deep breath, push down on your handlebars, and gradually return.

Take a deep breath and return to your room. Open your eyes and stretch. (pause) Take a few moments to appreciate the good feelings that come with relaxation.

Discussion

What does it mean to feel confident? What are some things you can do when you don't feel confident? Would you like to share the first message you wrote?

Activities

• Create a yellow brick road to success. Write a goal on a piece of yellow construction paper cut to resemble a brick. Place your bricks on the floor as a path. Classmates may wish to put all the bricks together and build a road of classroom goals.

• Develop a word web. Write your goal in the center of a piece of paper. Enclose the idea in an oval. Outside the oval write actions that you can do to achieve your goal. Connect the sub-topics to the oval by drawing lines between the action and goal.

• Design the perfect bicycle. Create an advertisement for your bike.

Books To Share

Jang, Molly. *Delphine*
McLeod, Emilie Warren. *The Bear's Bicycle*
Say, Allen. *The Bicycle Man*

Star Gazing

Objective

To provide children with a review of relaxation techniques, while continuing to use their imagination.

My mind is creative and free.

Script

Sit comfortably with your feet on the floor and your eyes closed. Take three long, deep breaths. (pause) Feel yourself relaxing more and more with each breath. Let the rhythm of the music calm you. Feel your muscles relax and your heart and breathing slow. Say to yourself, "I am calm and relaxed."

Take another breath and see yourself as a passenger in a limousine. You are in a special kind of limo with a glass top. Feel your body sink into the plush seat as you become calm and relaxed. It is late afternoon and you are expecting a long ride. Adjust your seat belt. Reach next to you, pull the lever back and feel your seat tilt back. Listen to the soft music playing and feel totally relaxed as you gaze out the glass top of your limousine.

The gray sky above slowly becomes darker and darker. (pause) Notice the shape of the moon as it becomes brighter and brighter. Focus in on the planet Venus, the first small light in the sky. It's soft glowing light relaxes you. (pause) Breathe in deeply. Slowly, stars begin to pop out at you. As you become more relaxed and concentrate on the sky, more and more stars appear.

Your thoughts are now lost in the layers of stars above. The black velvet sky is bursting with bits of bright light. The heavens give you a beautiful safe and warm feeling. Breathe slowly. You feel light-headed and playful. See the big dipper and little dipper. Play dot to dot with the stars and create your own constellations. With your eyes, draw pictures of things that make you happy. (pause)

Breathe slowly and say to yourself three times, **"My mind is creative and free"**. . . If you look with your mind you can see many new and wonderful things. Ask your driver to turn around and head home.

Take a deep breath and return to your room. Open your eyes and stretch. (pause) Take a few moments to appreciate the good feelings that come with relaxation.

Discussion

What images were the clearest? Does a person have to be smart in school to be able to be creative? What does creativity mean to you?

Activities

• Make a dot-to-dot constellation picture (for older children) or a starry night picture (for younger children) by sticking dots (stars) on a paper. Gaze at the dots and connect them to make a picture or design.

• Make a large star. Draw your favorite things on it. Hang the star from the ceiling.

• Make a "Twister" like game using various size labeled circles representing the sun and the nine planets. Instruct the children one at a time to start on Earth. Give them directions to challenge their balance and coordination. e.g."Put one hand on the sun, put the other hand on Saturn, put one foot on Neptune, put the other foot on Mars."

Books to Share

Keats, Ezra Jack. *Regards to the Man in the Moon*
Kandoian, Ellen. *Under the Sun*
Heckman, Philip. *The Moon is Following Me*

R
E
L
A
X

Learn

Expand the 3 R's to include a fourth— R.E.L.A.X. The following exercises help children develop academically.

Rainbow Wear

Objective

To help children achieve relaxation by linking a visual image with relaxation.

Script

When I am relaxed my body and mind work well.

Sit comfortably with your feet on the floor and your eyes closed. Take three long, deep breaths. (pause) Feel yourself relaxing more and more with each breath. Let the rhythm of the music calm you. Feel your muscles relax and your heart and breathing slow. Say to yourself, "I am calm and relaxed."

Take a slow, even breath. You are sitting under your favorite tree. Look on the ground and see that it has just rained. Breathe in and smell the damp, wet air. Everything around you has taken a bath. The grass seems healthy, happy and ready to grow. An ant comes out from hiding in the dirt. Follow the ant as it makes the long trip up a long blade of grass. When he reaches the top he stops, looks around, then takes a drink from a tiny bead of water. As he returns to the ground you wonder what it must be like to be an ant in a rainstorm.

Smell the flowers . . . the leaves . . . the dirt. They are alive and wide awake after the refreshing rain. The thirsty ground had so much to drink that small puddles have formed around you. Look into one of the puddles and see your reflection. You feel calm and relaxed. Look back into the puddle and over your shoulder. See a beautiful rainbow.

Look up into the sky and see it filled with bands of red, orange, yellow, green, blue, indigo and violet. The sun warms you. The rainbow amazes you with its beauty that fills the sky. You wish this rainbow could last forever. Take a breath and decide to keep this rainbow with you always. Reach up and take strips of color from the rainbow. Use these strips to weave a colorful, magical yarn. Breathe slowly. Take a small piece of this yarn and tie it around each ankle and feel your feet and legs become warm, calm and relaxed. Continue to slowly breathe. Take a longer piece of your yarn and tie it around your waist like a belt. Any nervousness you had in your stomach disappears. Tie a rainbow piece around each wrist. Feel the muscles in your fingers and arms relax.

Make a headband with your magic yarn and place it around your forehead. Your mind becomes relaxed and open to new thoughts. You are able to better remember things you have learned. Breathe slowly and repeat to yourself three times, **"When I am relaxed my body and mind work well..."** (pause) Pretend to have a piece of the magic rainbow yarn with you at all times.

When you need to relax take it out and use it. The rainbow in the sky is fading away.

Take a deep breath and return to your room. Open your eyes and stretch. (pause) Take a few moments to appreciate the good feelings that come with relaxation.

Discussion

What visual images help you relax? Why? Why do you sometime need to remind yourself to relax?

Activities

• Use multicolored yarn and braid it to make a headband, bracelet or ankle bracelet. Play soft music and sway holding rainbow colored streamers.

• Use a mixture of food coloring and rubbing alcohol to color different types of macaroni. Use rainbow pasta to create a mosaic picture, or thread the pasta onto a piece of yarn to make a rainbow necklace.

• Make an outside rainbow by spraying a fine mist from a hose into the air. Have children record the results of the experiment with drawings or paintings of the rainbow.

Books To Share

Ehlert, Lois. *Planting A Rainbow*
Freeman, Don. *A Rainbow Of My Own*
Hillert, Margaret. *Run To The Rainbow*

Music

I Know The Colors in the Rainbow by Ella Jenkins

Bubble Blowing

Objective

To help children appreciate themselves and feel more confident about remembering things.

Script

My mind holds many ideas.

Sit comfortably with your feet on the floor and your eyes closed. Take three long, deep breaths. (pause) Feel yourself relaxing more and more with each breath. Let the rhythm of the music calm you. Feel your muscles relax and your heart and breathing slow. Say to yourself, "I am calm and relaxed."

Breathe slowly. You are in a room which is totally quiet. There is nothing around to distract you. Listen...there is nothing to hear. Look...there is nothing to see. You are alone. You feel calm and relaxed. Clear your mind of all thought. Take a deep breath and as you breathe out, see, hear and think of nothing.

Concentrate on the words calm and relax. Spell them in your mind. C A L M, calm, R E L A X, relax. (pause) Take a deep breath. Breathe out, and in your mind blow a bubble just large enough for the words calm and relax to fit inside. Let the word bubble float around in your mind. The bubble will not float too far away. It is clear, so you can see and remember the words inside. This is a special bubble which will not pop until you want it to. Look up in your mind and see the words calm and relax.

Now think of a word that describes something good about you. (pause) Take a breath. Breathe out, and in your mind blow another bubble and put this good word inside. Let the bubble go into your memory knowing that you can call it back at any time. Concentrate on something a teacher taught you at school today. Something you want to remember. Take a breath and blow that thought into a bubble. Remember that you can make the bubble any size you wish. Release this bubble in your mind. Your mind and body are calm and relaxed. Being relaxed keeps the bubbles close by, the words easy to remember.

There are three bubbles gently floating in your mind. Each one has a thought you would like to remember. Breathe slowly. In your mind see the first bubble. The words, calm and relax, are still there for you to use. (pause). Call back the second bubble. Say to yourself the good word which describes you. (pause) Bring back the last bubble. Look through the clear round outsides and remember something you learned today. (pause)

You have many thoughts and ideas floating in your mind. Continue breathing slowing and repeat to yourself three times,

"My mind holds many ideas...". (pause) It is easier to remember things when your mind and body are relaxed. Your mind holds many ideas. All you have to do is let them out.

Take a deep breath and return to your room. Open your eyes and stretch. (pause) Take a few moments to appreciate the good feelings that come with relaxation.

Discussion

Why is it easier to remember things when you are relaxed? Could relaxing your mind and body help you on a test?

Activities

• Make bubbles. Mix 2 cups of water and 4 tablespoons of glycerine. Make dippers for the bubbles by cutting out the center of plastic lids such as those on margarine containers, or use the plastic baskets in which strawberries are packed.

• Using a paper cup, punch a small hole just large enough for the straw to fit in about one inch from the bottom of the cup. Push a straw through the hole. Use a small piece of clay and reach inside the cup and seal any openings around the straw. Put a small amount of water in the cup. Add liquid detergent and food coloring. The children may blow through the straw, forming bubbles which will come out of the cup.

Book To Share:

Zubrowski, Bernie. *A Children's Museum Activity Book*

A Walk In The Rain

Objective

To develop within children confidence in their ability to remember things they have learned.

Script

I remember what I learn.

Sit comfortably with your feet on the floor and your eyes closed. Take three long, deep breaths. (pause) Feel yourself relaxing more and more with each breath. Let the rhythm of the music calm you. Feel your muscles relax and your heart and breathing slow. Say to yourself, "I am calm and relaxed."

Breath slowly. You are just about ready to leave your house for school. Grab your umbrella, because the weather looks strange. As you walk to school, you notice that the air is perfectly still. There are large oval-shaped shadows on the street and sidewalk. Look up and see huge, fluffy white clouds hanging low in the sky directly above you. Something soft lands on your nose and tickles it. Soon the air is filled with white feathers drifting gently to the earth. As you watch the floating feathers, you feel calm and relaxed. Lay your head on the soft feathers. (pause) Take a deep breath and as you release it continue your trip to school. You hear a loud rumble in the sky. Look up and see huge, bright pink clouds overhead. Rainbow-colored lightning bolts fill the sky. Watch as the glitter hits the sidewalk all around you. It begins to rain glitter of every imaginable color. The glitter rain helps you notice the beauty of everyday things. The flowers seem to come alive with color. Their smells pour into your nose. Rub your hand over the green grass, and feel its thick texture. Smell the damp earth that helps the grass grow. Lay down in the soft grass, relax, and enjoy the little things around you. (pause)

As you breath slowly, another giant cloud forms overhead. Soon it begins to rain letters of the alphabet. As the letters come down, they become words, then sentences. Look up and imagine that in the sky is a giant book of facts, filled with all the things you have learned.Lay back, and repeat to yourself three times, **"I remember what I learn..."** (pause) Take a deep breath and as you release it notice that you have arrived at school. You enjoyed your trip immensely. Your mind is filled with many wonderful and important things. Come back to this special place whenever you need to remember things and open the book.

Take a breath and return to your room. Open your eyes and stretch. (pause) Take a few moments to appreciate the good feelings that come with relaxation.

Discussion

Why is it easier to remember things when you are relaxed? What are some strategies you use to remember things?

Activities

• Describe a thunderstorm so that someone who has never experienced one would know what a storm is like.

• Find an old cap and decorate it with buttons, pins, paint, glue or glitter. Call it your thinking cap and wear it when you want to remember something.

• Give each child a small paper cup containing alphabet macaroni. Ask them to spell words. After everything is cleaned up and put away, ask them to write down what words they spelled with the macaroni.

• Make raindrops out of paper. Write important spelling, vocabulary or other words and hang them on the ceiling. Invite children to do this at home using study words. Variation: Hang positive words about themselves on the ceiling over their bed. Read these words before going to sleep each night.

Books To Share

Barrett, J. *Cloudy With A Chance Of Meatballs*
Brown. *Arthur's Teacher Trouble*
Friedrich P. *The April Umbrella*
Gibbons, Gail. *Weather Forecasting*

Exploration

Objectives

To help children improve their ability to use their imaginations and provide a positive message about opportunities to explore and learn.

Script

I enjoy learning new things.

Sit comfortably with your feet on the floor and your eyes closed. Take three long, deep breaths. (pause) Feel yourself relaxing more and more with each breath. Let the rhythm of the music calm you. Feel your muscles relax and your heart and breathing slow. Say to yourself, "I am calm and relaxed."

Find yourself sitting on the sidewalk on a warm day, looking at an ant. All your attention is focused on this little creature as it zigs and zags—zags and zigs. Your insect friend now finds a crumb of food and begins to slowly carry it around. You are lost in thought as you watch the show in front of you. Feel calm and relaxed and at peace with the world around you. Watch the ant disappear into a crack in the sidewalk.

Take a deep breath. As you exhale, make yourself small, and follow your friend down his little hole. You are in a new world, a world you never knew existed. See the darkness slowly become light, as your eyes get used to your new surroundings. Find an old coin that was lost a hundred years ago. Touch it and think of who might have dropped it. (pause) How did your neighborhood look a hundred years ago? (pause) Now see an arrowhead. Rub your thumb back and forth over its side. In your mind, create a story about how this particular arrowhead was used. (pause) Take a deep breath, and go deeper. Find a fossil that is as old as time. What did the animal look like? Picture it in your mind. (pause) Find something else very old on your underground trip. Use your imagination to discover what it is. (pause)

Feel calm and relaxed in your new world. Breathe slowly and repeat to yourself three times, **"I enjoy learning new things"**... (pause) Look up and see a crack of bright light above you. Head back to the surface. Feel yourself growing back to your normal size. There are so many exciting things for you to explore and learn about.

Take a deep breath and return to your room. Open your eyes and stretch. (pause) Take a few moments to appreciate the good feelings that come with relaxation.

Discussion

What else did you find on your underground trip? What would you like to explore or learn about this school year?

Activities

• Take a "texture" walk to feel a variety of objects. Do a "rubbing" picture.

• Hold an old object in your hands and close your eyes. Imagine the object when it was new. Imagine who owned this object. What did the world look like? How can an old object teach us something new?

• Ask an older person to talk about the history of your area. Ask them what things were like when they were your age.

• Using a magnifying glass or microscope look at dirt and dust. What new things did you learn?

• Ask children to bring in a small jar of dirt. Compare and contrast the collections. Grow something in the dirt.

Books To Share

Sadler, Marilyn. *Alistair's Time Machine*
Hall, Donald. *Ox Cart Man*

Calvin and Hobbes   by Bill Watterson

Lost Land

Objective

To encourage children to explore new opportunities.

Script

Where there is an
opportunity for learning,
I explore it.

Sit comfortably with your feet on the floor and your eyes closed. Take three long, deep breaths. (pause) Feel yourself relaxing more and more with each breath. Let the rhythm of the music calm you. Feel your muscles relax and your heart and breathing slow. Say to yourself, "I am calm and relaxed."

You are on an ocean beach. Feel the sea breeze cool your face. Watch the waves rise and fall, charge and retreat. Listen as they slurp and slop the shoreline. You are standing barefoot in warm, white sand. Feel the sand wrap around your feet massaging your heel and toes. Concentrate on your toes and feel them relax. Lift one foot and feel the sand sift down between your toes. Lift the other foot and experience the sand running down between your toes. Sit down. Wiggle your fingers in the warm soft sand. Feel your hands and then arms relax. Lay down. Feel your whole body conform to the beach. Each particle of sand is like a pillow relaxing your entire body. Feel the warmth of the sand. Feel the soothing vibrations of the ocean water. Breathe in deeply. You are totally calm and relaxed. (pause)

Sit up and look around. Something is very different about the beach now. You must have dozed off. The tide has gone way, way out exposing a whole new world right in front of you. The ocean has dried up all the way to an island that has been covered with water for thousands of years. You look all around, decide that it's safe, and begin to explore. The ocean floor is like another world. Smooth rocks and sea shells make beautiful patterns at your feet. As you head for the island you encounter colorful coral formations. Red, orange, blue, pink and purple, the coral has woven itself into beautiful sculptures. One looks like a pink dinosaur. See another large piece. What does it look like to you? (pause)

Find a starfish on a rock in front of you. He is standing on one leg and waving the other four trying to get your attention. He says that all the other marine life has followed the water away but he has stayed to guide you on your journey. Give him a name. (pause) As you and your new friend walk, the coral forms a tunnel leading directly to your destination. As you set foot on the island you know that people must have lived here a long time ago. Find some shells with holes drilled in them. These were probably once used for necklaces. Imagine how the people looked.

(pause) Find a small triangular piece of broken pottery. What did their dishes look like? (pause) Find some round, smooth stones with some lines cut into them. What were these strange stones used for? (pause) Find an old rusty anchor. What type of ships sailed to the island? (pause)

There are no diamonds or gold buried on this island, just little clues to a land that once was. It was certainly worth the trip. Breathe slowly and repeat to yourself three times, **"Where there is an opportunity for learning, I explore it..."** (pause) Take a deep breath and as you breath out the water comes back. Find a large flat piece of wood and ride it like a surf board back to the beach. Exploring and asking questions are very good ways to learn. You can solve mysteries if you look for the clues.

Take a deep breath and return to your room. Open your eyes and stretch. (pause) Take a few moments to appreciate the good feelings that come with relaxation.

Discussion

What new opportunities for learning have you had this year? What opportunities do you hope to explore?

Activity

• Think about goals for yourself. Think of a goal for tomorrow, next week, next month and next year. Write down your goals on your calendar. You may want to tell someone about your goals or you may want to keep them to yourself.

Books To Share

Seuss, Dr. *Oh The Places You'll Go*
Wyler, Rose. *Seashore Surprises*

Inspiration

Objective

To encourage children to use writing as a way to express themselves.

Script

I can express myself through writing.

Sit comfortably with your feet on the floor and your eyes closed. Take three long, deep breaths. (pause) Feel yourself relaxing more and more with each breath. Let the rhythm of the music calm you. Feel your muscles relax and your heart and breathing slow. Say to yourself, "I am calm and relaxed."

You are alone in your room, sitting at your desk, with pencil and paper in front of you. All is quiet, except for the soft music you hear faintly in the background. Concentrate on the music. Lean back in your chair, and feel your toes relax, feet relax, legs relax, seat relax, waist relax, chest relax, arms relax, and neck relax. Your entire body becomes calm and free of tensions. (pause) The music relaxes your mind and releases the creative energy that is within you.

Reach out and pick up your pencil which lies on your desk. It rests comfortably in your hand. As you touch your pencil, it glows a light green color. Feel the pencil warm and soothe your fingers. Feel this energy flow up your arm and stimulate your entire body. As you press your pencil to the paper, the sun peaks through your window. The sun reflects through the glass and forms a rainbow of light on your paper. Red, yellow, green, blue, violet, all the beautiful colors, light your way as your pencil glides. The words flow as the rainbow directs your writing instrument. Feel the creative energy of your mind travel through your arm and onto the paper. Enjoy the feeling as your hand makes large loops and small loops. You are finding just the right words to write. Your thoughts become wonderful words for all to see. Your printed words will last a long time.

Repeat to yourself three times, **"I can express myself through writing..."** (pause) Put your imaginary pencil down. Remember your pen or pencil is glowing just waiting to help you express yourself.

Take a deep breath and return to your room. Open your eyes and stretch. (pause) Take a few moments to appreciate the good feelings that come with relaxation.

Discussion

What are some advantages of writing your thoughts as opposed to just saying them? Does relaxing music help you when you work or study?

Activities

• Take a minute to begin a poem, a short story, or any type of writing you want. Don't forget to enjoy what you have written because it comes from you and is unique.

• Imagine that you are your favorite author. You have just been asked to write another book. What will the book be about?

• Decorate your own special pencil. Tie on colorful strips of ribbon or yarn to make rainbow streamers. Use this pencil for special writing projects.

Book to Share

Wood, Audry. *Quick as a Cricket*

Listen

Objective

To reinforce the positive trait of being a good listener.

Script

I am a good listener.

Sit comfortably with your feet on the floor and your eyes closed. Take three long, deep breaths. (pause) Feel yourself relaxing more and more with each breath. Let the rhythm of the music calm you. Feel your muscles relax and your heart and breathing slow. Say to yourself, "I am calm and relaxed."

You are walking on wet sand where the water washes the beach. It is a warm, sunny summer day. Feel the cool, refreshing sand ooze between your toes. Sit down in the sand, and feel it massage your legs and seat. As you breathe in deeply, the water rises to wash and relax your lower body. Breathe deeply and slowly as the waves roll in...and out...in...out...in...out. Put your hands in the wet sand, and feel them relax. The sand relaxes your fingers, palms, wrists and releases tension in your arms and upper body. Make a handprint, and watch it as it slowly fills with water. Now it disappears back into the crystal white sand. You are calm and relaxed. You begin to notice the many seagulls around you. They soar and dip without moving their wings, using only the cool lake breeze for energy. Hear one sea bird, now many birds, as they glide in the sky in search of food. Listen for the other sounds by the sea. What do you hear? (pause) When you are quiet and relaxed, you can notice more sounds that surround you.

Look down and see a large conch seashell next to you. It is bumpy on the outside, but pink and shiny on the front and inside. Pick it up and press the cool, smooth part against your ear. Hear the relaxing sound of the waves lapping the shore. Listen closely, and hear soft music in perfect rhythm with the waves. Now, listen again, and try to hear a message just for you. (pause) Whisper to yourself three times, **"I am a good listener...."** (pause) Put down the shell. Being a good listener helps you to enjoy and appreciate the world around you. Being a good listener also helps you to be a good student and friend.

Take a deep breath and return to your room. Open your eyes and stretch. (pause) Take a few moments to appreciate the good feelings that come with relaxation.

Discussion

Why do people like good listeners? What are some things you could do to become a good listener?

Activities

• Sit quietly and listen to the sounds surrounding you. Concentrate on just one sound and then imagine the world without that sound. What would the world be like?

• Turn out the lights and have children become aware of all the sounds that can be heard. Someone may produce a sound and others guess what it is they are hearing.

• Play the "telephone game" where a message is whispered from person to person around a circle.

• List or web ideas for different categories of sounds: e.g. country, city, inside, outside.

• Bring a conch sell or other shell to pass around the group. Listen to the sound of the "sea."

• Visit a river, lake or ocean. Keep a list of all the sounds. Record the sounds and play them when you return home. Close your eyes and pretend you are back by the water.

Books to Share

Lubell, C & W. *By the Seashore*
Fowler, Allan. *Hearing Things*
Rius, Maria. *Hearing*

Finding Treasure

Objective

To encourage children to develop a positive feeling about reading books.

Script

Reading will help me learn wonderful things.

Sit comfortably with your feet on the floor and your eyes closed. Take three long, deep breaths. (pause) Feel yourself relaxing more and more with each breath. Let the rhythm of the music calm you. Feel your muscles relax and your heart and breathing slow. Say to yourself, "I am calm and relaxed."

See yourself sitting in a hot tub. The water is perfectly warm. Lean back and relax. Notice the ripples in the water as they flow up and down...up and down. Feel your feet become light and float up to the top. Light streaks of steam wiggle up from the water and disappear in the air. Breathe in this steam. Feel it dance in your nose. Now fill up your lungs with warm soothing air. Air is pushed out from pipes in the hot tub. This air causes an underwater current, a stream of relaxation. Put your feet in this current. Feel any tension in your muscles drift away. Put your back in this magic current. Feel any remaining stiffness evaporate in the warm soothing water. Now put into the current any other part of your body that is tense. You feel totally relaxed.

Dive in and discover a magical sea underwater. Begin to explore. You can breathe underwater. You are in an undersea world of magnificent beauty. Swim past the bright red and green vegetation. Glide by beautiful formations of purple and orange coral. As you near the bottom you notice objects shining like diamonds. Upon closer inspection you notice the diamonds are really pretty shells of every shape and size. The shells form a line which leads you to a treasure chest. Breathe slowly and easily...and open up the chest. The treasure is books, many books all with beautiful covers. You cannot wait to read them all! Open the largest book to find a very important message. Repeat this message to yourself three times, **"Reading will help me learn wonderful things..."** (pause) Books are treasures with so much information buried inside. Put this book under your arm and swim toward the surface. Don't forget to enjoy the scenery. Come to the top and take a deep breath.

As you exhale return to your room. Open your eyes and stretch. (pause) Take a few moments to appreciate the good feelings that come with relaxation.

Discussion

What was your favorite book when you were younger? What do you like best about going to the library? If you were an author, what type of book would you write?

Activities

- Design a cover for the book about your life.
- Organize a neighborhood or school book exchange.
- Make a treasure chest out of a cardboard box. Put your favorite books inside.

Books to Share

Gibbon, G. *Sunken Treasure*
Trelease, J. *The Read-Aloud Handbook*

Book Adventure

Objective

To instill in the students a sense that they can have a positive influence in their lives.

Script

Reading can take me anywhere.

Sit comfortably with your feet on the floor and your eyes closed. Take three long, deep breaths. (pause) Feel yourself relaxing more and more with each breath. Let the rhythm of the music calm you. Feel your muscles relax and your heart and breathing slow. Say to yourself, "I am calm and relaxed."

It's a warm windless day and you are sitting on a blanket under a gigantic oak tree holding a book. Breathe in and smell your favorite outside smell. This smell makes you calm and relaxed. Open the book and see something very strange. Some of the letters seem to be wiggling back and forth as if they are talking to each other. Now watch as each letter R breaks free and runs down the page. Soon all the letters begin to move. Watch as they march off the page, down your leg and under your blanket. You are surprised and disappointed. Take a deep breath and let it out slowly. As you breathe out jump into the book and become a part of the story yourself.

You are standing in a huge white paper field. Look up into the white sky and see thousands of words floating by like clouds on a summer day. Streaks of bright colors light up the sky like fireworks. Breathing slowly, think of a place in your favorite book. Watch as the colors drip down from the sky and paint this place all around you. (pause) Think of your favorite character from a book. (pause) The character walks out of the scenery and stands right next to you. Travel with this character on a short adventure. (pause)

As you are traveling repeat to yourself three times, **"Reading can take me anywhere..."** (pause) Imagine how many places you can go and people you can meet through books. Look back up into the sky and find the words "the end". Throw a rope around them and swing out of the book.

Take a deep breath and return to your room. Open your eyes and stretch. (pause) Take a few moments to appreciate the good feelings that come with relaxation.

Discussion

What was the last good book you read? Why is reading good

exercise for your mind? If you could own just one book, which one would it be? Why?

Activities

• Give each child an animal cracker. Have them develop a short story with that animal as a character.

• Read a book to someone who is younger than you.

• Write a different ending to a favorite story or book.

• Read a chapter per night after dinner with your family. Predict what you think will happen next.

• Make a poster to try to sell your favorite book. Why is it a "must-read"?

• Design a book jacket for your favorite book.

• Write a letter to the author of a book telling them what you liked best about the book. Write the authors of this book. We'd love to hear from you!

• Make a diorama of a scene or a far away place described in a book you have read.

• Read and learn about children who live in other countries. On a world map mark the countries you have visited through books.

Test Preparation

Achievement Tests—Day 1

Objective

To help students attain their best possible performance on group tests. This will be achieved by having them visualize performing well and maintaining relaxation during testing.

Script

Sit comfortably with your feet on the floor and your eyes closed. Take three long, deep breaths. Feel yourself relaxing more and more with each breath. Let the rhythm of the music calm you. Feel your muscles relax and your heart and breathing slow. Say to yourself, "I am calm and relaxed."

As your breathing slows down imagine that today is the day to take your group achievement tests. You feel confident and relaxed and look forward to the challenge. Taking tests helps you to think about remaining calm, confident and relaxed.

Imagine your teacher passing out the test booklets. Watch them come to your desk. As each booklet is passed out you become more and more relaxed. Feel the tension drain from your body. If you notice any tension or anxiety simply take a deep breath and say to yourself, "I am calm and relaxed." As you relax you gain more confidence.

The test booklet is on your desk. The teacher asks you to open it to the first page of instructions. Each turn of the page is a signal for you to relax. Now see yourself reading the test instructions and complete the sample questions. Your teacher tells you it is time to begin the first test. The first test is _____. Do the easiest questions first, and then come back to the harder ones. Notice how you stay relaxed by breathing slowly. When you notice yourself getting worried or anxious you simply take a deep breath and say the words, "calm and relax". If you are not sure which one is the correct answer you make the best guess by reading the question with each possible choice and choose the one that makes the most sense. Once you have completed each item, you see yourself going back over each to check your answers. To you, testing is becoming easier because of your ability to stay relaxed.

The next test is called _____. Again see yourself carefully reading the sample question. Stay relaxed, breathing slowly. Feel your arms and shoulders relaxing even more. Go to your special place and say to yourself, "I am confident and relaxed. I enjoy the challenge of taking achievement tests. I try my hardest. I stay relaxed. When I don't know the correct answer, I make the best guess possible. I check my work."

Today's test is over. You have done the best you can do and feel proud of your hard work. You compliment yourself for taking your time, staying relaxed, and following directions. Open your eyes now and get ready to listen to your teacher.

Discussion

Why is it important to stay relaxed during tests? What steps should you take if you feel yourself getting worried or tense?

Test Preparation

Achievement Tests—Day 2

Objective

To help students remain relaxed while completing group achievement tests.

Script

Sit comfortably with your feet on the floor and your eyes closed. Take three long, deep breaths. Feel yourself relaxing more and more with each breath. Let the rhythm of the music calm you. Feel your muscles relax and your heart and breathing slow. Say to yourself, "I am calm and relaxed."

As you breath slowly and exhale feel your whole body let go of any tension. Arms and shoulders relaxed. Hands and fingers warming. Relax your neck and all the muscles in your face. Feel the relaxation spread to your chest, stomach and hips.

Relax your legs. Let go of any tension in your ankles and feet. As you continue to relax, let yourself drift with the music. Take a deep breath and as you let it out slowly, imagine your teacher telling you that it is time to take more achievement tests. You stay calm and relaxed. You feel confident and know what to expect. Breathing slowly, relaxing. Be aware of any tension that sneaks into your body and release it by relaxing that area.

Now in your mind picture your teacher passing out the test booklets and see yourself staying relaxed. Your teacher tells you to open your test booklets. When you open your test you feel even more relaxed. You feel confident and relaxed.

Today's tests are _____. On each section you read the directions carefully. Next see yourself completing the sample questions. Finally see yourself reading the questions while staying relaxed. Imagine a great book of facts in your special place. When you feel stuck simply say to yourself, "relax and calm" and go to your special place. Imagine the book of facts which contains all of the things you have learned. You feel confident about the answer you choose.

Breathe slowly and stay relaxed. During each time you take tests you will do your best. Stay relaxed by being aware of your breathing. Slow breathing, calm and relaxed. Tonight at home practice relaxing by releasing all the tension in your muscles. Open your eyes and listen carefully to your teacher.

Discussion

Why do schools give achievement tests? Why do some children get nervous before tests? What are some things you plan on doing if you feel nervous?

Test Preparation

Achievement Tests—Day 3

Objective

To help students remain relaxed and feel confident about completing group achievement tests.

Script

Sit comfortably with your feet on the floor and your eyes closed. Take three long, deep breaths. Feel yourself relaxing more and more with each breath. Let the rhythm of the music calm you. Feel your muscles relax and your heart and breathing slow. Say to yourself, "I am calm and relaxed."

Take one more breath and slowly release it. Imagine your teacher telling you that the last day of testing is today. The word testing signals you to relax. Let go of all the tension in your body. Relax your upper body. Release any tension in your face, neck, shoulders, arms, hands, fingers. Relax your lower body. Legs relaxed. Feet relaxed. As you become more relaxed imagine your teacher passing out the test booklets.

Today's tests are _____. You feel confident and relaxed. See yourself open your test booklet and stay relaxed. See yourself read the instructions carefully. See yourself complete the sample questions. See yourself staying relaxed and completing the entire test. Complete each item by looking carefully at all the possible answers. You feel confident that the answer you choose is the correct one. Say to yourself three times, "I am relaxed and confident about taking tests."

Open your eyes and be ready to listen to your teacher.

Discussion

Discuss any questions students may have about the upcoming achievement tests.

Test Preparation

Achievement Tests or General Testing

Objective

To provide a brief relaxation exercise in preparation for taking a test.

Script

Sit comfortably with your feet on the floor and your eyes closed. Take three long, deep breaths. Feel yourself relaxing more and more with each breath.

Let the rhythm of the music calm you. Feel your muscles relax and your heart and breathing slow. Say to yourself, "I am calm and relaxed."

Take a deep breath and as you release it relax even more. In your mind, look over your test. You are feeling calm and relaxed, as you now see yourself looking in the book of facts.

When you look in this book, you can find all the answers you need. Take a deep breath, and relax. You are confident that you can do well on today's test.

Take a deep breath, and open your eyes.

The book of facts is open.

You may go back to it whenever you need.

Discussion

Why is it important to tell yourself that you will do well on tests?

R
E
L
A
X
Appreciate

*These scripts focus on appreciation of
self and the world around.*

Good News

Objectives

To have children appreciate and imagine themselves as being unique and special. To reinforce the key words calm and relax.

Script

I am good news.

Sit comfortably with your feet on the floor and your eyes closed. Take three long, deep breaths. (pause) Feel yourself relaxing more and more with each breath. Let the rhythm of the music calm you. Feel your muscles relax and your heart and breathing slow. Say to yourself, "I am calm and relaxed."

The room is quiet, as you slow your breathing. Your seat now transforms into your favorite soft lounging chair. On your lap is today's newspaper. On page one, in big, bold print, it says, "You are CALM and RELAXED." When you see or hear these words, you feel calm and relaxed. Below these almost magic words, there is a picture of a young person who has done something special. Look closer at the picture, and find that this person is you! You are the news today. You have done something unique.

You have used a special talent that you have to achieve a goal, a dream. You are a winner, a heroine or hero, a hard worker, who has earned recognition in the newspaper. Breathe slowly and read the good things about you. (pause) How are you feeling? (pause) Repeat to yourself three times, **"I am good news."**. . . (pause) Close the newspaper. You have many talents and with patience and hard work you can make some of your dreams come true. Next time you see a newspaper, think of your good news.

Take a deep breath and return to your room. Open your eyes and stretch. (pause) Take a few moments to appreciate the good feelings that come with relaxation.

Discussion

How did it feel to read the good news about yourself? What was the good news about yourself? Share something good you imagine yourself doing this year.

Activities

• Make your own newspaper with an article about a Very Important Person - YOU! Include articles that talk about your special interests and talents.

• Find five words in a newspaper that describe you.

• Find each letter in your name and write a word that describes you for each letter.

Pillar Of Strength

Objective

To link a visual image with the feelings and self-statement of being important to oneself and others.

Script

I am important to myself and others.

Sit comfortably with your feet on the floor and your eyes closed. Take three long, deep breaths. (pause) Feel yourself relaxing more and more with each breath. Let the rhythm of the music calm you. Feel your muscles relax and your heart and breathing slow. Say to yourself, "I am calm and relaxed."

Imagine that you are a telephone pole. You are high off the ground. As your breathing slows you start to feel calm and relaxed. The breeze rocks you gently back and forth, back and forth, back and forth. Look up and see the soft white clouds moving ever so slowly across the clear blue sky. Feel the top of a tree tickle you as it brushes against your wood. It is a beautiful day and you are calm and relaxed. Listen to the birds as they fly around you. One has chosen to land on you and rest. Once you were home to a nest of birds. You feel secure when you look forward and backward and see the many telephone lines you help to hold up. The wires are like your arms connecting you to others many miles away. You reach out and touch someone. You feel proud knowing how important you are. Many people appreciate and depend on you.

Breathing slowly, you sway in the breeze feeling calm and relaxed. You are tall, you are strong, you are relaxed. Repeat to yourself slowly three times, **"I am important to myself and others."** . . . (pause) Next time you see a telephone pole, stand tall knowing how important YOU are.

Take a deep breath and return to your room. Open your eyes and stretch. (pause) Take a few moments to appreciate the good feelings that come with relaxation.

Discussion

How do telephone poles depend on other telephone poles? If telephone poles had feelings, why might one pole feel like it is not important? In what ways can you be important to others?

Activities

• Read *The Giving Tree* by Shel Silverstein. Discuss the similarities to the script above.

Pumpkin Patch

Objective

To help children appreciate and accept differences in people.

Script

Everyone is unique.

Sit comfortably with your feet on the floor and your eyes closed. Take three long, deep breaths. (pause) Feel yourself relaxing more and more with each breath. Let the rhythm of the music calm you. Feel your muscles relax and your heart and breathing slow. Say to yourself, "I am calm and relaxed."

Picture yourself alone in the countryside. The trees are green and yellow—some have magnificent patches of red. The leaves rustle around you. The autumn breeze makes some leaves dance at your feet. It is chilly, but your jacket gives you warmth and security. Breathe slowly and enjoy the good feeling that comes with peace and relaxation. Your eyes, nose - all your senses are enjoying this country walk so much that you lose track of time. You see yourself in the middle of a huge pumpkin field. There is orange as far as you can see.

Feel yourself becoming tired and sitting on a large sturdy pumpkin. You take time to notice each pumpkin around you. All the pumpkins are different. See a large round one. See a long thin pumpkin. Here is one that's oval shaped and almost yellow. See a short fat one hugging the ground. One almost looks like the number eight. Even pumpkins from the same vine are different.

You are calm and relaxed as your mind wanders. You have always thought all pumpkins were round and orange. You too are different from other people. People are different even within the same family. Breathe slowly and say to yourself three times, **"Everyone is unique. . . ."** (pause) You are different and unique. There is not another person just like you.

Take a deep breath and return to your room. Open your eyes and stretch. (pause) Take a few moments to appreciate the good feelings that come with relaxation.

Discussion

What is prejudice? Why do some people dislike others who are different? What can you do to stop prejudice? Why are differences in people important?

Activities

• Think of things that might seem the same yet actually are very different—for example, pumpkins, leaves, snowflakes, twins. Each person in your group may want to design a pumpkin or a snowflake.

• Provide each student with paper to cut out a snowflake. Design a bulletin board with the heading "All Beautiful and All Unique" and attach the children's snowflakes to the board.

• Visit a pumpkin farm. Notice the different colors, shapes, and textures of pumpkins. Write about the trip.

• Design pumpkins without stems and hang them on a wall. Using a blindfold play "tape the stem on the pumpkin."

Books To Share

King, Elizabeth. *The Pumpkin Patch*
Steptoe, John. *Mufaro's Beautiful Daughters*
Dahlov, Ipcar. *Bring In the Pumpkins*

Attic Visit

Objective

To help children appreciate the value of memories.

Script

I have many good memories.

Sit comfortably with your feet on the floor and your eyes closed. Take three long, deep breaths. (pause) Feel yourself relaxing more and more with each breath. Let the rhythm of the music calm you. Feel your muscles relax and your heart and breathing slow. Say to yourself, "I am calm and relaxed."

Breathe slowly and evenly, and imagine you are standing in your attic. Sit down on an old chair in the corner. It is perfectly quiet and you feel calm and relaxed. It is dim but not dark. Notice the minute dust particles as they dance across the rays of sunlight. Breath in the old but sweet air.

Look around the room. See some of your favorite old toys propped up against the posts. Clothes are hung from the rafters. Seeing these old things relaxes you. Enjoy this feeling. Enjoy the quiet time by yourself. Now go over to a dusty old trunk in the corner. The hinges creak as you slowly pull open the top. What is inside makes you feel very good.

Take a relaxing breath and enjoy your favorite old toy or outfit which is contained in the trunk. Pick it up and hold it close to you. This object has many beautiful memories attached to it. Relax and enjoy your time alone with your memories. Think of how good this object makes you feel (pause). Now carefully put your special item back into the trunk. Breathing slowly, repeat to yourself three times. . . **I have many good memories. . . .** (pause) Remember that you can visit your attic whenever you want and hold onto your special memories.

Take a deep breath and return to your room. Open your eyes and stretch. (pause) Take a few moments to appreciate the good feelings that come with relaxation.

Discussion

What are some of your good memories? Why do good memories help us relax when we are upset? Why is it important to remember the past? If you could travel into the past what year would you choose to visit? What would you take with you? What would you bring back?

Activities

• Share a personal memory with a child about something that was special to you when you were younger.

• Introduce historical fiction books that include stories about children.

• Draw a picture of a favorite toy from your past. Where is it now? How far back in your life can you remember?

Books To Share

Flournoy, Valerie. *Patchwork Quilt*
Lund, Doris Herold. *Attic of the Wind*
Williams, Margery. *The Velveteen Rabbit*
Bahr, Mary. *Memory Box*

Get Away

Objective

To help children develop a positive strategy to deal with worries.

Relaxing can help me solve problems.

Script

Sit comfortably with your feet on the floor and your eyes closed. Take three long, deep breaths. (pause) Feel yourself relaxing more and more with each breath. Let the rhythm of the music calm you. Feel your muscles relax and your heart and breathing slow. Say to yourself, "I am calm and relaxed."

You are outside on a clear summer day. You are lying on your back in the tall cool grass thinking about many things. Some things are worrying you. Look up and see a huge white fluffy cloud drift over you. Study it with your eyes and your mind. It has hundreds of interesting rounded curves and indentations. It is like nothing you have every seen before. The cloud is beautiful, quiet and peaceful. You wish you could live on this cloud. Take a deep breath and feel yourself becoming light-headed.

Reach up and feel yourself lift off the ground. Take one last very deep breath, reach higher and as you release your breath you find yourself resting on the soft calmness of your own private cloud. If you still feel a little heavy, wrap yourself in the light white air of the cloud. Spread it on any part of your body to relax it.

Explore your new world. The view below is fantastic. Look down and see a little dot that you believe is where you live. You wonder if anyone down below can see a little dark speck in your cloud and know it is you. Using your hands make cloud snowballs and throw them in all directions. Each one becomes a unique little cloud. Decorate the sky with clouds. (pause) Float over a dark blue ocean. Look up and see nothing but blue sky. Look down and see nothing but blue water. It is perfectly silent. You are totally at peace. (pause)

Say to yourself three times, **"Relaxing can help me solve problems. . . ."** (pause) Out of the top part of your cloud fashion a huge sail and turn it so you begin to drift back home. Look down and see your little green field. Feel yourself get heavier and heavier. Your cloud slowly drops and lands softly in the green grass. Wave your hand and send your cloud back to the heavens for someone else to use. Call your cloud back when you need to get away for a while and think about good things.

Take a deep breath and return to your room. Open your eyes

and stretch. (pause) Take a few moments to appreciate the good feelings that come with relaxation.

Discussion

While you were floating on your cloud what were some of worries you solved? How could "floating on a cloud " help you deal with worries?

Activities

• Take a blue piece of paper. Fold it in half. Put a blob of white paint on one side of the paper. Refold the paper and press the two sides together. Open it and look at your cloud.

• Using white construction paper, tear out the shape of a cloud. Make a list of words that describe feelings. Circle the words that describe the way you feel today. Write a feeling mobile to hang from the ceiling.

• Write a story about an imaginary trip. Include destination, companions and an aerial view of the earth.

Book to Share

DePaola, Tomie, *The Cloud Book*

One Of A Kind

Objective

To help children appreciate their uniqueness.

Script

There is only one person in the world like me.

Sit comfortably with your feet on the floor and your eyes closed. Take three long, deep breaths. (pause) Feel yourself relaxing more and more with each breath. Let the rhythm of the music calm you. Feel your muscles relax and your heart and breathing slow. Say to yourself, "I am calm and relaxed."

Picture yourself on a small island somewhere far from home. The sun is shining brightly. A cool ocean breeze wraps around your body and relaxes it.

Sit down on a large smooth stone and look around your island. Notice how beautiful it is. You also realize that there is something odd about this place but can't quite decide what it is. The island has only one tree. Look up at the tall palm. The breeze makes the long branches dance and appear as if they are waving at you. Listen as the wind moves through leaves. It makes the sound of a thousand whispers.

The tree is home to one bright blue parrot with a long orange beak. At the top of its trunk hangs one large ripe furry coconut. In the other direction is the one mountain on the island. A small stream winds down the mountain then explodes into a rainbow waterfall. Listen, try to hear the water as it crashes and splashes on the rocks below. (pause)

At the foot of the mountain is a small crystal blue lake. Your island is paradise but something still feels strange. Look in the other direction and see a magnificent red flower with a black and yellow center. It seems to be the only flower on the island. You see one cactus, one cave, one cloud in the sky. What is going on here? Even though the island is so beautiful it is also so very different. Suddenly the rock on which you are sitting begins to slowly shake, then rises into the air.

Look down and see that your rock has sprouted four legs and a head. You are not afraid when you realize that you are on the back of an old tortoise. The tortoise lifts his head high and tells you that if you scratch behind his ears he will tell you the secret of the island.

Reach out and touch his head. It feels cool and rough. The tortoise begins to walk. You slowly rock back and forth. . .back and forth. . .back and forth. . . You feel calm and relaxed. Look out and see one rabbit, one snail, one butterfly. Say to yourself "There is ONLY ONE of everything on this island." The old tortoise slowly lifts up his head, looks at you and says that you have discovered the secret. In a low slow voice he tells you that because there is only one of everything on the island everyone can be themselves, be an individual. The wise old tortoise smiles and says he will give you a secret to take back with you. Repeat this secret to yourself three times, **"There is only one person in the world like me. . ."** (pause) You do not always have to try to be like someone else. You are different. You are unique. You are one of a kind. Be yourself.

Take a deep breath and return to your room. Open your eyes and stretch. (pause) Take a few moments to appreciate the good feelings that come with relaxation.

Discussion

Why is it sometimes hard to be different than someone else? In what way is it good to be different?

Activities

• Design a coat of arms. Include something you enjoy doing, a hobby, something important to you, etc.

• Trace around your hand. Use your imagination to create handy art.

• Look at the end of your fingers with a magnifying glass. You will see patterns that are uniquely yours. Press a child's thumb into an ink pad. Then press the thumb unto a piece of paper. Make a series of thumbprints. Design characters from them. Draw faces onto the thumbprints to show feelings such as happy, unhappy, anger, worried, sad. Write/tell a story about the characters.

Books To Share

Emberly, Ed. *Ed Emberly's Great Thumbprint Drawing Book*
Lessac, Franne. *My Little Island*

Self Sculpture

Objective

To help children appreciate themselves as unique, changing individuals.

Growing and changing can be good for me.

Script

Sit comfortably with your feet on the floor and your eyes closed. Take three long, deep breaths. (pause) Feel yourself relaxing more and more with each breath. Let the rhythm of the music calm you. Feel your muscles relax and your heart and breathing slow. Say to yourself, "I am calm and relaxed."

You are a large block of ice standing outside on the sidewalk. It's a cold but sunny day. Suddenly it gets darker. Feel extra weight pressing down on top of you. People walking by are sitting on you to rest. You are sturdy and just the right height. Enjoy the warm and secure feeling that your company provides. Soon everyone who passes takes a minute to sit and relax on you. You feel warm, relaxed and useful. Take another deep breath. Look up through your ice and see someone walking around looking at you from every angle. Hear the noise of a hammer and chisel.

Feel the tingling sensation as little pieces are chipped off your block. Begin to feel lighter. The sun is warming new parts of your body. You can see much clearer now. You are being fashioned into an ice sculpture. The sun dances inside of you and reflects as if you were a giant diamond. You feel tall, free and energized. People stop and admire your beauty. Take a slow, steady breath and imagine yourself as a magnificent ice sculpture. What are you? (pause) Take another slow, deep breath and feel yourself becoming warmer and lighter. Feel a mild breeze wrap around you. Smell the fresh new air. Hear the birds sing. Feel the drops of water tickle as they run down your arms and legs.

Flow down the sidewalk, down a hill and into a clear rushing stream. You are water and free to flow. Enjoy the feeling as you bubble over rocks, swirl around twigs and slide down miniature water falls. People are sitting on benches watching the clear blue stream and enjoying all the signs of spring. As you bob and weave you feel the current getting stronger. You are now part of a mighty river full of energy and power.

Breathe in deeply and as you exhale say to yourself three times, **"Growing and changing can be good for me"**. . . (pause) Gather yourself. No matter what shape you are in, or how you look on the outside, you are important and ever changing.

Take a deep breath and return to your room. Open your eyes

and stretch. (pause) Take a few moments to appreciate the good feelings that come with relaxation.

Discussion

What form of water did you most enjoy being in the story today? What are some important qualities you possess? What changes have you recently noticed about yourself?

Activities

• Choose one beautiful thing you can see in the winter. Describe your winter wonder.

• Make snowflakes from coffee filters. Flatten a coffee filter. Fold the filter in half, then fold in thirds (a triangle will be formed). Design a unique snowflake by cutting notches in the sides, top and bottom of the folded filter. The snowflake may be decorated using diluted glue and glitter.

Books To Share

Baylor, Byrd. *Guess Who My Favorite Person Is*
Brown, Margaret Wise. *The Important Book*
Carle, Eric. *The Mixed Up Chameleon*
Knudson, R.R. *Rhinehart Lifts*

Mysterious Music

Objective

To encourage children not to judge people before they have had an opportunity to get to know them.

Script

I learn about people before I judge them.

Sit comfortably with your feet on the floor and your eyes closed. Take three long, deep breaths. (pause) Feel yourself relaxing more and more with each breath. Let the rhythm of the music calm you. Feel your muscles relax and your heart and breathing slow. Say to yourself, "I am calm and relaxed."

You are home, lying in bed. Put the book you are reading on the nightstand. Reach up and turn off the lamp. Fluff your pillow, and get your covers just the way you like them. Feel your heart rate slow, your breathing slow, as you become more and more relaxed. Listen to the complete quiet in your bedroom. (pause) Notice a faint sound coming from far away. Concentrate on the sound. (pause) It seems like music, but it's an instrument that you have never heard before. The music starts low and then goes high. Each beautiful note seems to come from a different instrument. You decide to find the source of this wonderful noise. Put on your clothes, grab a flashlight, and begin to explore.

The night is still. Even the crickets must be listening. A warm fog covers the earth. The beam from your flashlight seems to pull you along. Notice some very strange footprints. Each track is a different size and shape. All have a flower growing in the middle. A trail of glitter winds around the tracks and lights up when the flashlight shines on it. The musical sound is getting louder. The crickets and owls now seem to be singing along. Lean against a tree and listen to this beautiful song. The music relaxes you and gives you a peaceful feeling. Feel yourself begin to doze off. (pause)

Look up through the fog and see before you the alien who has been making the music. At first you're afraid, but something inside you says to walk closer to the creature. The alien is very different looking, with many tiny odd-shaped feet. The feet not touching the ground are playing strange musical instruments. You are curious and not afraid. The alien is covered with black scales and has a long tail with golden glitter at the tip. His face is full of pimply-like red spots. He reaches out and gives you one of his instruments, and you begin to play it. Soon, you become very good friends. You talk all night and learn about each other. He teaches you many things about his planet.

Breathing slowly, look this creature in his eight eyes, and repeat to yourself three times, **"I learn about people before I judge** them. . . ." (pause) You've just had a very exciting dream. You remember to not judge people on how they look, because who knows, they could become your very best friend. In fact your friendship could be out of this world.

Take a deep breath and return to your room. Open your eyes and stretch. (pause) Take a few moments to appreciate the good feelings that come with relaxation.

Discussion

Have you ever been misjudged by someone? What are some ways you can learn about someone? What does it mean when they say, "You can't judge a book by its cover and beauty is only skin deep?"

Activities

• Read this poem and discuss:

> *We can make a special day*
> *When we think of things to share.*
> *Little acts of kindness*
> *Will show others that we care.*

• Listen to a tape of an instrumental piece of music without words. While you are listening, write words or phrases describing the pictures that come to mind.

• Share the story of The *Ugly Duckling.* Ask the children if they've ever felt like the duckling. Discuss how others can affect the way we see ourselves. Talk about believing in yourself no matter what others say. Follow up by having students begin an ongoing log of their own feelings.

Books To Share

Cosgrove, Steven. *Kiyomi*
Lionni, Leo. *Fredrick*
Walter, Mildred. *Ty's One Man Band*

Endless Stream

Objective

To encourage children to share themselves and their things with others.

Script

Sharing with others makes me feel good.

Sit comfortably with your feet on the floor and your eyes closed. Take three long, deep breaths. (pause) Feel yourself relaxing more and more with each breath. Let the rhythm of the music calm you. Feel your muscles relax and your heart and breathing slow. Say to yourself, "I am calm and relaxed."

You are standing in a green grassy field on a beautiful summer day. Take a deep breath, and smell the clear, crisp air. Notice the crystal blue sky. See a yellow buttercup wildflower next to you. Bend down, take a deep breath, and feel the flower's sweet fragrance fill your lungs and entire body. You feel calm and relaxed. Listen closely, and hear the breeze crackle the leaves of the mighty oak trees in the distance.

You can also faintly hear the sound of running water. You decide to investigate. As you walk closer to the sound of the water, you discover a very small stream shaped like many letter S - es, one after another. Sit down, take your shoes off, and dangle your feet in the cool moving water. Throw a white stone into the clear stream, and watch as it wiggles down to the bottom. Throw another in the stream. Watching it weave in the water, then rest on the bottom, relaxes you. Throw another small stone . . . throw another . . . and another.

A brownish-colored bottle floats by and gets caught on a stick directly in front of you. Watch the bottle as it bobs up and down, up and down. (pause) As you look closer at the bottle, you notice it has a label on it. The label says, "If you want a wonderful surprise, open this bottle." Reach down and take it from the water. Take a deep breath. Pull the cork from the bottle as you exhale and sit back and wait for your surprise. Nothing happens. Hold the bottle up in the air. It catches the breeze just right and begins to produce beautiful sounds. The sounds get louder and turn into music. Listen. . .(pause) Feel the bottle begin to shake in your hands. Out of it comes a magnificent stream of rainbow colored light. Red, yellow, green, blue, violet. . .all your favorite colors. The sky is filled with magic. As the rainbow continues to come out, use the bottle as a spray can, and write your name in the sky. Lay back and enjoy it all. Find some empty bottles on the bank next to you. Catch pieces of the rainbow, and put them inside these bottles. Don't forget to put the corks in.

At first, you want to take the bottles home and collect them, but you decide rainbows should be spread for all to see. Start putting the bottles filled with rainbows into the stream. Watch as they slowly bob and swirl and finally flow out of sight. Imagine the bottles moving from the stream to a river, then all over the world through the oceans. Breath slowly and repeat to yourself three times. . ."**Sharing with others makes me feel good. . .**" (pause) You feel energized when you think of other children opening your bottle and sharing your beautiful rainbow.

Take a deep breath and return to your room. Open your eyes and stretch. (pause) Take a few moments to appreciate the good feelings that come with relaxation.

Discussion

Some children in our country do not have a home. They carry their belongings with them from place to place. What three things of your own could you give a homeless child in order to make his or her life easier?

Activities

• Brainstorm (web) ways to share things in the home, in school, in the community.

• Capture the beautiful colors of the rainbow in a collage by making a suncatcher for your window. Tear colored tissue paper scraps into small pieces. Put the scraps between two pieces of waxed paper. Seal the waxed paper by pressing with a warm (not hot) iron. Tape your suncatcher to a window.

Book to Share

Balian, Lorna. I *Love You, Mary Jane*

Calvin and Hobbes

by Bill Watterson

Around The World

Objective

To help children develop an attitude of acceptance and appreciation of people who differ from them.

Script

All people on earth have many things in common.

Sit comfortably with your feet on the floor and your eyes closed. Take three long, deep breaths. (pause) Feel yourself relaxing more and more with each breath. Let the rhythm of the music calm you. Feel your muscles relax and your heart and breathing slow. Say to yourself, "I am calm and relaxed."

Your vacation has just begun. You have traveled to a country so new that it does not yet have a name. Check to see if your camera is loaded with film. You are carrying a back-pack for souvenirs from your trip. As you begin to stroll down the cobblestone Main Street you notice the beauty of this city. Look up and see huge colorful banners draped from the buildings. The long blue banner has the world "Welcome" written on it. The green banner hanging from the theater says "Welcommin". The orange one says "Bienvenidos". There are hundreds of these colorful banners and each one says "welcome" in a different language. Take a picture of this magnificent sight.

As you continue to walk you notice the many smells that fill the air. Breathe in deeply and smell the sweet smell of French pastry. Now breath in the spicy smell of Italian pizza. Breathe in and smell Chinese vegetables sizzling in their woks. Breathe in and smell your favorite smell in the whole world. Feel it fill your entire body. You feel calm and relaxed. Imagine what it would be like to have a gigantic feast of all the wonderful foods in this city. As you continue your adventure you hear what seems to be a different language coming from each house. Put on magic headphones which allow you to understand what the people are saying. A German family is planning a picnic. A Mexican family is talking about a soccer game on T.V. An African family is making a gift for Grandma. They are talking about many of the same things you talk about with your family and friends.

The people now realize that they have a visitor in their land. They come out and each one gives you a little gift. Each family is dressed differently and their skin is a different color. They welcome you and say you may stay as long as you wish. A parade is being planned in your honor. Take one last picture of the beautiful place. As you look through your camera, you see what a small world we really have. Breathe slowly and repeat to yourself three times, **"All people on earth have many things in common. . . ."**

(pause) Even though people may look different and speak different languages, they have the same feelings that you have.

Take a deep breath and return to your room. Open your eyes and stretch. (pause) Take a few moments to appreciate the good feelings that come with relaxation.

Discussion

Have you ever met a person from a different country or different part of the United States? What things did you have in common with them? Share your experiences. Have you ever traveled to a different country? What was it like? If you could live anywhere in the world, where would you pick to live?

Activities

• Plan an ethnic meal/snack.
• Collect stamps from around the world. Locate the countries on a map. Write a message telling about an imaginary trip the stamp has taken.
• Talk about the country where your ancestors once lived.

Books To Share

Brisson, Pat. *Magic Carpet*
Dorros, Arthur. *This Is My House*
Krupp, Robin Rector. *Let's Go Traveling*
Levinson, Riki. *Watch The Stars Come Out*

Surprise Season

Objective

To help children anticipate change in themselves by linking this thought with a visual image of changing seasons.

Script

Seasons change and so do I.

Sit comfortably with your feet on the floor and your eyes closed. Take three long, deep breaths. (pause) Feel yourself relaxing more and more with each breath. Let the rhythm of the music calm you. Feel your muscles relax and your heart and breathing slow. Say to yourself, "I am calm and relaxed."

Take a relaxing breath and picture yourself outside raking leaves. It is a cold November day and you are wearing a warm jacket, hat and gloves. Listen as the wind rattles through the empty trees. Watch as the wind swirls a few leaves around your feet. Raking is hard work, but the exercise keeps you warm. Pull the brown leaves toward you stroke after stroke, (pause) stroke after stroke. Rest now. Take a deep breath and feel the air soothe your arms which ache from raking.

You feel calm and relaxed as you look at the many piles of leaves you have made. Your body is warm and you feel ready to finish the job. As you continue, the rhythm and sound of the rake brushing against the ground relaxes you. Reach and pull, (pause) reach and pull, (pause) reach and pull. (pause) The pile becomes bigger and bigger. Now set your rake against a tree. Run and jump in the gigantic pile of leaves. The leaves become a warm blanket as they surround and relax your body. Enjoy this feeling of relaxation.

As you lay on your back, look up into the gray sky. Something wet hits your nose. Something cold and wet hits your cheek. You now feel cold spots on your forehead. Sit up and look around. There are big white SNOWFLAKES landing all around you! The leaf piles are already dotted with white. Soon a fluffy blanket of snow will cover the entire yard. You are surprised at this display of natures beauty. Should you put your rake away and get a shovel?

Breathe in deeply the cold fresh air and repeat to yourself three times, **"Seasons change and so do I. . ."** (pause) Everything changes, including you.

Take a deep breath and return to your room. Open your eyes and stretch. (pause) Take a few moments to appreciate the good feelings that come with relaxation.

Discussion

What are some changes you have made since last year that surprised you? What are some changes you might go through this year?

Activities

• Find or draw pictures of yourself from the time when you were a baby and put them on a time line or make a personal photo album.

• Observe or chart changes in nature. Example: If a tree is available, mark a leaf and go outside twice weekly and observe the color changes by coloring pictures with colored pencils.

• Observe a caterpillar turn into a butterfly.

• Build a snowman and watch it over several days. Draw it or take pictures each day and make a timeline using the pictures.

Books To Share

Bauer, Caroline Feller. *Midnight Snowman*
Carle, Eric. *The Very Hungry Caterpillar*
Hader, Berta and Elmer. *The Big Snow*
Watson, Wendy. *Has Winter Come?*

Drawer Full of Memories

Objectives

To develop an appreciation for important people in our lives and to link an image of a loved one with a feeling of love and joy.

Script

I feel love and joy in my life.

Sit comfortably with your feet on the floor and your eyes closed. Take three long, deep breaths. (pause) Feel yourself relaxing more and more with each breath. Let the rhythm of the music calm you. Feel your muscles relax and your heart and breathing slow. Say to yourself, "I am calm and relaxed."

You are sitting at a desk in your bedroom. You are very much alone and all is quiet. Lean back, feeling calm and relaxed. Take a moment to enjoy the good feeling that comes with relaxation. Reach over and open a drawer in your desk. Inside this drawer are many old photographs that bring back warm, pleasant memories. Pick out one photo and lay it on the desk. It is a picture of you and a person who is special to you doing something together. Take a deep breath. Think of a good time you've had with that special person (pause). Open the long skinny top drawer of your desk. Look past the pencils, rulers, and paper clips and find a souvenir - something you've saved from a special trip or visit. Is it a rock, a button, a postcard, a sea shell, or some other item? Hold on to this item. Breathe in deeply and remember this special outing as you slowly exhale.

You are feeling calm and relaxed as you open the large bottom drawer in your special desk. Look inside and take out a gift you have received from a friend or loved one. Think about who gave you this gift. (pause) Continue to breath slowly and feel secure knowing that right outside your bedroom door are people who care about you. Think of a friend or family member and say to yourself three times, **"I feel love and joy in my life. . . ."** (pause) Close the drawer in your desk. Take a deep breath, return to your room and open your eyes. Remember to say thank you or I love you to those closest to you.

Discussion:

Who came to your mind? What are some things that make this person special? Is it possible to find at least one person who cares about you? How would you seek someone out if you felt that no one cared about you?

Activities

• Gather some things that are special to you. Display them and tell others about them. Make a "Me" poster. Include pictures of your family doing things together.

• Draw a large calendar with a square for each day of the week. Write a positive happening on the square for that day.

• Research your family history and make a family tree.

• Designate a VIP (Very Important Person) area. Ask a child to bring in pictures or objects that describe them.

• Pass around a hand mirror and recite the following poem:

I looked inside my looking glass,
To see what I could see.
I guess I must be happy today,
Because that smiling face is me!

Books To Share

DePola, Tomie, *Now One Foot, Now the Other*
Joose, B. *Mama, Do You Love Me?*
Joose, B. *I Love You The Purplest*
Flournoy,V. *The Patchwork Quilt*
Munsch, R. *Love You Forever*
Rylant, Cynthia. *The Relatives Came*

Music

Raffi, "All I Really Need"
Neuman, Randy, "Family" (from *James and the Giant Peach*)

R
E
L
A
X-pand

Explore the possibilities of R.E.L.A.X.
These suggestions will help you expand
your knowledge and usage of the
program.

Pleasant Dreams

Objective

To provide an imagery-guided, relaxation exercise with a suggestion for using positive thinking before falling asleep.

Script

I go to sleep easily at night.

Sit comfortably with your feet on the floor and your eyes closed. Take three long, deep breaths. (pause) Feel yourself relaxing more and more with each breath. Let the rhythm of the music calm you. Feel your muscles relax and your heart and breathing slow. Say to yourself, "I am calm and relaxed."

It's been a busy day, but now it's time to get ready for bed. Hear the doorbell ring. You walk to the door, open it, but find no one there. Look down and see a rectangular box lying on your front step. Next to it is a small box in the shape of a triangle. Both are wrapped in paper that changes color before your eyes. As you carry in the packages, they feel warm and mysterious. Take a relaxing breath, and begin to untie the ribbons around the rectangular box. Fold back the tissue paper, and see a pair of red slippers in your size and in the latest style. Sit down, slip them on, and lean back to look at the slippers on your feet. Breathe in slowly, and begin to relax.

As you become more relaxed, the slippers begin to change color. Take another breath, concentrate on your feet, and experience the feeling of relaxation. As you relax, the color of your slippers continues to change.

Breathe in slowly and deeply, and feel the tension completely leave your toes . . . feet . . . ankles . . . calves . . . knees . . . and thighs. When your lower body is totally relaxed, your slippers will change into your favorite color. Reach down, and lift the next layer of tissue paper from the box. Discover a beautiful robe, fit for a king or queen. As you hold it up in front of you, notice its beautiful color and design. The robe is woven from shiny golden thread. Put one arm in the robe, and feel its security and comfort as your arm relaxes. Put the other arm in, and it, too, relaxes.

Take a breath and hold it. Pull the magic robe over your shoulders, and button it as you release your breath. The golden thread soaks up the light in the room and warms your arms . . . shoulders . . . and chest. Enjoy the feeling as your upper body is totally free of tension. You are calm and relaxed.

Reach down, and open the triangular box. Inside is a beautiful sparkling hat shaped like a cone. Put the hat on your head. This hat lets your mind relax and funnels in only happy, peaceful thoughts. There are so many good things about you to think about. Take a moment to think about one thing good about you. (pause)

Now it's time to turn off the light and go to sleep. Breathe slowly, and say to yourself three times, **"I go to sleep easily at night . . . "** (pause) Take a relaxing breath and slowly let it out. The person who left the magic clothes by your door wanted to tell you something. Each night before you go to bed, look at your robe or pajamas, and think about one good thing you did that day. You go to sleep with positive thoughts and sleep well and wake up refreshed.

Take a deep breath and return to your room. Open your eyes and stretch. (pause) Take a few moments to appreciate the good feelings that come with relaxation.

Discussion

Why does it help to create a positive thought while trying to fall asleep? What are some examples of positive thoughts you could use tonight? If someone were to deliver a package to your door with something to help you relax, what would be in it?

Activities

• Make a special nightshirt to wear to bed. Use an oversized T-shirt and washable fabric paints.

• Play "Pass the Package" game. Sit in a circle like musical chairs. Pass a wrapped gift box around. When the music stops the child holding the box describes something she/he could do that could help him/her relax.

Books To Share:

Hoban, Russell. *Bedtime For Frances*
Mayer, Mercer. *There's A Nightmare In My Closet*

Fish Story

Objectives

To provide children with the message of the importance of having patience and to keep trying.

I have the patience to keep trying.

Script

Sit comfortably with your feet on the floor and your eyes closed. Take three long, deep breaths. (pause) Feel yourself relaxing more and more with each breath. Let the rhythm of the music calm you. Feel your muscles relax and your heart and breathing slow. Say to yourself, "I am calm and relaxed."

You are standing by a small, beautiful lake. It's a lazy summer day and you are alone with your fishing rod and a can of bait. Walk by the shore. Hear the small waves lap the shoreline. Feel the sun beat down on your head and arms. See the sunlight up the sparkling water. Breathe in deeply and smell the fresh lake breeze. Notice a faint smell of fish. This smell lets you know that there are fish to catch. You want to catch a big one.

Find a grassy hill near the water. Look up to see a huge shade tree to keep you cool. This is the perfect spot to sit, rest and get your fishing line wet. Put corn or any other bait on your hook. Set your red and white bobber so your hook goes all the way to the bottom. Throw your line in a perfect spot. Sit down in front of the big tree, lean back and relax. Feel your heartbeat and breathing slow down. Watch your bobber drift slowly back and forth. It moves gently up and down, causing small circular waves. Follow one of these waves until it disappears by the shore. (pause)

Notice for the first time the echoing of birds. As you follow the birds, notice that the sun is directly overhead. The exact time of day does not matter because you have left your watch and worries behind you. You feel totally calm and relaxed watching your bobber float. Find some pebbles next to you. As you throw them in the water listen to the different sounds they make. Listen to a tiny pebble. Listen to a medium-sized one. Now throw in a large pebble and hear its sound as it hits the water. Find a flat rock and skip it across the lake. Count the skips. (pause)

The sun is going down. The sky becomes orange. Birds dive and skim the water looking for food. Crickets begin to chirp. Hear the low sound of a frog on a lily pad. Reel your fishing line in slowly. You are a little disappointed that you did not catch any fish. You feel at peace and enjoyed your quiet time alone with nature. As you lift your line from the water you notice a message attached to your hook.

Breathe slowly and read this note to yourself three times, **"I have the patience to keep trying . . . "** (pause) This message makes you feel proud that you did not give up even though you did not catch any fish. Remember to keep trying.

Take a deep breath and return to your room. Open your eyes and stretch. (pause) Take a few moments to appreciate the good feelings that come with relaxation.

Discussion

Think of a time you showed patience and kept trying and share it with the class. What are some positive steps you can take when you start to feel frustrated?

Activities

• Make a list of 10 uses of fishing line. Do you have the patience to list all of them that come to mind?

• Drop a pebble in a bucket of water. Follow the circular waves and describe what happens. Vary the size of the bucket and the objects dropped.

• Role play situations where patience is required.

Going Places

Objective

Children will gain an appreciation of the outdoors and the values of exercise. Participation, not winning, is stressed.

Script

Exercise helps me feel better.

Sit comfortably with your feet on the floor and your eyes closed. Take three long, deep breaths. (pause) Feel yourself relaxing more and more with each breath. Let the rhythm of the music calm you. Feel your muscles relax and your heart and breathing slow. Say to yourself, "I am calm and relaxed."

You are outside on a chilly morning. Take a breath. Let it out and watch your breath becomes steam as it mixes with the cold air around you. Breathe in as deeply as you can. Breathe out and make an even larger cloud of steam.

Watch the steam as it disappears into the air above. Take another breath. Breathe out as much steam as a large locomotive. As it evaporates you feel calm and relaxed. You are out for your daily walk in the park. You are alone with your thoughts. The sun is just peeking over the tree tops, making long thin shadows all around you. The rising sun makes the colors of nature richer and more beautiful. As you walk, notice the sparkling dew on the emerald grass and the newly fallen orange and yellow leaves. As you pass the deep blue pond see a thin cloud of steam hug the calm water. All is quiet except the chirping birds who greet the morning with busy sounds. Listen . . . As you continue to walk you breathe slower and slower.

The path soon becomes crowded. First tens, then hundreds, then thousands of people are headed to some mysterious place. The park paths are full, you cannot move forward anymore. People are starting to line up in back of you. Stand on your tiptoes and look ahead. See at least ten thousand people in bright colored sweatsuits stretching, talking and laughing. Squint your eyes and look far ahead to see a huge banner with the word "START" printed on it. Over a distant loudspeaker hear the word "GO". There is a race today and you are participating. The people in the far away front of the line begin to bob up and down as they move forward. The line stretches out as more and more people jog forward. Like a giant wave, people slowly move ahead. Finally the others around you begin to inch forward.

Breathe deeply, walk and then begin a steady jog. Feel the energy of all those around you. Concentrate on the music. Move with the rhythm, getting stronger and stronger with each step. The cool air soothes your chest and lungs with each breath. Your pace is comfortable and invigorating. Even though you have traveled this way before you notice new things about the scenery that surrounds you. Breathe slowly and repeat to yourself three times, **"Exercise helps me feel better . . . ."** (pause)

The finish is ahead. You have run a nice even race. The people who are already done and the spectators applaud as you cross the finish line. You feel proud of yourself. Someone comes over and puts a gold medal around your neck. Everyone receives one. Everyone who exercises is a winner. The prize is not a medal but a better feeling about yourself. Try to do some form of exercise every day.

Take a deep breath and return to your room. Open your eyes and stretch. (pause) Take a few moments to appreciate the good feelings that come with relaxation.

Discussion

What is your favorite outdoor activity? Why does exercise help you relax? What is the farthest you have run or walked? The first Olympic Games took place in Athens, Greece. If you could design a children's Olympics, what events would you include?

Activities

• Brainstorm different ways of exercising. Set up a personal exercise plan and keep a log of your progress describing different ways you exercise each day.

• Organize a group walk through the neighborhood.

• Develop a relay race where all team members are important and everyone has an equal chance.

• Pledge to be healthy. Talk about the desire for a happy healthy life. Talk about the qualities of a healthy life. Compose a personal pledge including elements that reflect your goals. Write your pledge on a piece of paper and sign and date it . "Age" the paper by blotting it with a damp tea bag. When dry, roll the paper in a tube. Tie a ribbon around the scroll. Keep it in a place where you can frequently reread your pledge.

Books To Share:

Aesop. *The Tortoise and The Hare*
Berenstein, Jan and Stan. *The Big Race*

Hidden Beauty

Objective

To introduce the concept that we have the ability to find beauty in most anything, if we make an effort to do so.

Script

I always look at the positive side of things.

Sit comfortably with your feet on the floor and your eyes closed. Take three long, deep breaths. (pause) Feel yourself relaxing more and more with each breath. Let the rhythm of the music calm you. Feel your muscles relax and your heart and breathing slow. Say to yourself, "I am calm and relaxed."

Picture yourself standing around a small odd-shaped evergreen tree. The snow covers your boots and numbs your toes. The wind is blowing and your cheeks are red. The tree you have chosen is one of the last ones on the lot. It is bare and bent but full of possibilities. Shake the tree and watch a few of the needles litter the snow below. Bring the little tree home. Feel the warmth and security of your home. Take off your scarf, hat, gloves, boots and finally your coat. You feel calm and relaxed as you look at your little tree leaning proudly in the corner. As you breath deeply you notice the smell of pine needles. Study the tree. The more you look at it the better it gets. The tree would look best in front of the window for all to see. It stands straight up and it's branches seem to strengthen as you drape on the lights, tinsel and ornaments.

Concentrate on the music and think of a time when you decorated a tree. Remember the bright colors . . . , the holiday tastes and smells . . . , bells and other glorious sounds. Remember the warm and peaceful feelings you had. Feel calm and relaxed as you sit and look at the beautiful tree nature has made and you have decorated. (pause) Now plug in the bottom string of lights. The glow lights up the many packages beneath the tree. Plug in the middle lights and watch as the tinsel and ornaments seem to come alive and dance on the sturdy branches. Plug in the top lights and the ceiling illuminates warmth and contentment. Feel proud of your little tree. It's beauty and bright lights energize you. Breathe in deeply the pine scented air and say to yourself three times, **"I always look at the positive side of things . . . "** (pause) You have the power to find beauty in everything around you.

Take a deep breath and return to your room. Open your eyes and stretch. (pause) Take a few moments to appreciate the good feelings that come with relaxation.

Discussion

What does this statement mean, "Beauty is in the eye of the beholder"? Give some examples. Why is it important to try to find something positive even in a bad situation?

Activities

• Find something in your house that you don't use any more. Fix it up and give it to someone who would enjoy it.

• Adopt a small tree, bush or plant in your backyard or neighborhood. Nurture and protect it.

• Think of a tree that you are familiar with. Discuss how this tree helps other living things. Draw a picture of this tree during four different times of the year. Draw a picture of this tree in four different stages of its growth.

Books To Share

Brown, M. *The Little Fir Tree*
Keats, E. *Jennie's Hat*

Smoke Signals

Objective

To encourage children to tell someone if they are abused or deeply troubled.

Script

I tell someone I trust when I am hurt inside.

Sit comfortably with your feet on the floor and your eyes closed. Take three long, deep breaths. (pause) Feel yourself relaxing more and more with each breath. Let the rhythm of the music calm you. Feel your muscles relax and your heart and breathing slow. Say to yourself, "I am calm and relaxed."

It's a crisp clear autumn day and you are standing on a street corner. Rub your hands together to warm them up. You have nothing to do so you stare at the rooftop of a nearby house. Light gray smoke is rising from the chimney making designs in the dark blue sky. You imagine that the slanted roof is a Native American teepee with smoke signals coming out. Pretend they are in trouble and trying to get help. What message are they sending? (pause)

The noise of a loud truck driving by distracts you. Watch as the truck drives down the road. Thick black smoke rises up from the exhaust pipe. Watch as the ugly smoke snakes toward the sky. A smelly odor fills the air as you watch the truck disappear down the road. (pause)

You rub your hands together and stomp your feet to warm up. You now notice that you can see your breath. Take time to think about a problem you sometimes think about when it is quiet or you are alone. A problem that has been with you for awhile. (pause) Take a deep breath and as you exhale watch this problem come out like white steam. You feel better when you let this problem flow out of you for awhile. Take another breath and say to yourself three times, **"I tell someone I trust when I am hurt inside . . . "** (pause) Remember that it feels good to tell someone you trust when you are deeply hurt, bothered or in trouble.

Take a deep breath and return to your room. Open your eyes and stretch. (pause) Take a few moments to appreciate the good feelings that come with relaxation.

Discussion

Why is it good to tell someone your hurt feelings? Who are some people in your life that could help you with your problems?

Activities

• Make a list of people you could talk to if you had a problem at home or at school
• Role play sharing a troubling feeling with a parent or a friend.
• Your younger children sing this song to the tune of " If You're Happy and You Know It, Clap Your Hands."

If you're in trouble and you know it,
tell a friend.
If you're in trouble and you know it,
tell a friend.
If you're in trouble and you know it,
Then your face will surely show it,
If you're in trouble and you know it,
tell a friend.

Books to Share

Carle, Eric. *Mixed Up Chameleon*
Carlson, Nancy. *I Like Me*
Godwin, P. *I Feel Orange Today*
Howe, J. *I Wish I Were a Butterfly*
Murphy, J. B. *Feelings*
Shamat, M. *I'm the Best*
Steptoe, J. *Daddy Is a Monster. . . Sometimes*
Sanford, *I Know the World's Worst Secret*

Happy Landings

Objective

To help children develop an attitude of caring for their environment.

Script

Sit comfortably with your feet on the floor and your eyes closed. Take three long, deep breaths. (pause) Feel yourself relaxing more and more with each breath. Let the rhythm of the music calm you. Feel your muscles relax and your heart and breathing slow. Say to yourself, "I am calm and relaxed."

Picture yourself walking up a small mountain. A cool breeze is blowing in your face. Pump your arms as you walk up higher and higher. Breathe in deeply and feel the oxygen and energy fill your lungs. You are almost to the top. Feel the muscles stretch in the back of your legs. Tighten your leg muscles and release them. You have hiked to the top of the mountain and earned a little rest. Sit down and imagine that you are the king or queen of the hill. There are no people in your small mountain kingdom, but you rule over many animals and beautiful plants and flowers. Breathe in and feel calm and relaxed. Below you, right at your feet, is your favorite animal. Reach down and pet it. Feel it rub against your hand. All the animals are very tame and not afraid of you.

Now take into your arms an animal you always wanted to hold. (pause) A flock of birds make a circle around you. Each bird is a different bright and beautiful color. Each bird sings one clear note and together they perform magical music on your mountaintop. The music relaxes you and makes you a proud leader. Take a minute to enjoy your calm and relaxed feeling. (pause) Look up into the blue sky and see a bird flying toward you. As the bird comes closer it becomes larger. As it lands next to you, you recognize it as a very large, grand old eagle. He invites you to sit on his back and somehow you know that it is the right thing to do. The eagle has special feathers for you to hold on to as you take off. What fun it is to glide like a bird in flight. Feel and hear the air as your feathered friend turns into the wind, soars higher, higher and higher.

Your magic ride has taken you over the clouds into a strange but beautiful atmosphere. You slowly fly over a place with many types of birds, insects, fish and mammals that you have never seen before. Some look very strange while others are just a little bit different than the animals you have in your mountain kingdom at home. Your old eagle friend explains to you that these creatures once lived on earth but are now extinct and will never live there again. With a tear in his eye he tells you that eagles too might be gone from earth one day. Take a deep breath and repeat to yourself three times, **"I respect the earth and living things . . ."** (pause) The eagle flies you past your magic mountain and heads home. Take care of the air, water, and land so that all types of life can grow and be happy.

Take a deep breath and return to your room. Open your eyes and stretch. (pause) Take a few moments to appreciate the good feelings that come with relaxation.

Discussion

What are some things you do or could do to take care of the air, water and land?

Activities

• Next time you go for a walk, take along a bag and collect things that don't belong outside.
• Take a "listening" walk.
• Make a bird feeder. Put peanut butter on a pinecone and roll the cone in bird seed. Use a cookie cutter to cut a piece of stale bread into a shape. Brush with egg white. Sprinkle with bird seed. Hang it in a tree for the birds.
• Design a T-shirt with a logo/picture about the earth.

Poem To Read

Greedy little sparrow
Are you very hungry?
Great big crow
No place to go?
Saucy little chickadee
Come and eat my bread crumbs
All in a row.
In the snow.
　　　—Anonymous

Books To Share

Ashenbrener, Gerald. Jack, *The Seal and the Sea*
Cosgrove, Stephen. *Maui-Maui*

Something From Nothing

Objective

To encourage students to make use of their creativity and use time wisely.

Script

When I am bored, I find something to do.

Sit comfortably with your feet on the floor and your eyes closed. Take three long, deep breaths. (pause) Feel yourself relaxing more and more with each breath. Let the rhythm of the music calm you. Feel your muscles relax and your heart and breathing slow. Say to yourself, "I am calm and relaxed."

It's raining outside. The weekend is here and you are at home. The rain makes you think the "B" word. That word is bored. The rain has made you cancel your outdoor plans. Watch the raindrops collect on your bedroom window. The raindrops zigzag in little streams racing to the bottom of your window. Pick out a raindrop and watch it as it winds down the window pane, getting faster and stronger as it mixes with other drops of water. The glass is fogged up except for the areas the water has streaked down. Focus on the design on the window. Now focus on looking out the streaked window at the shades of grey outside. Concentrate on the sound of the rain as it hits your roof and window.

Hear the doorbell ring. Walk to the door and see that a long thin package has been delivered with your name on it. The rain has made the writing on the package run together, so you cannot tell where it came from. Cut the twine off the box. Next strip the tape, then unwrap the brown paper that surrounds the package. Slowly, take the top off the box. Inside is an odd-shaped piece of plastic. Also in the box are two wooden sticks, thin scraps of white cloth and a large ball of string. This is certainly not a treasure box. It is a box filled with junk.

As the rain continues to tap on the roof, you decide to make something from the items inside the package. Pick up the plastic and lay it on the floor. Breathing slowly you look at the plastic and wonder what it could become. (pause) After much thought, make a cross from the two sticks and lay it on the plastic. Cut small pieces of string and tie the cross down. Tie the strips of cloth together to make one long piece. Finally, tie the cloth strip to the bottom of the plastic and the end of the ball of string to the top. Get some magic markers and make colorful stars of all sizes on your creation.

You have worked so hard and long on your project that you failed to notice that the rain has stopped. Look out the window and feel the bright sunshine energize your entire body. Grab your project and run outside. As soon as you hit the fresh breeze your creation lifts toward the bright blue sky. Hold it by the ball of string. Feel it pull against your hands and arms. Everytime you pull down on the string, the object heads higher and higher. Give it more string until it reaches outerspace and then the stars.

With the help of a box full of junk on a rainy day, you have used your imagination to construct a beautiful kite. Take a deep breath and repeat three times, **"When I am bored, I find something to do . . . "** (pause)

If you tell yourself you are bored, you will feel that way and time will drag on. Use your imagination, create things and time will fly just like your beautiful kite.

Take a deep breath and return to your room. Open your eyes and stretch. (pause) Take a few moments to appreciate the good feelings that come with relaxation.

Discussion

Have you ever been stuck inside on a rainy day?

Have you ever said the words, "I'm bored" or "I have nothing to do?" When you are bored, what are some things you can do instead of watch TV?

Activities

- Design a kite bookmark. Cut a diamond shape from a 3x5 card. Color and decorate it. Glue a 12 inch piece of yarn to the back for the string. Choose a book to read and keep your new bookmark in it.
- Make a family commitment to turn off the TV. Talk together and decide if you are watching an appropriate amount of TV. Write a plan for one week. After a week evaluate your plan together.
- Where does your time go? Make a chart of your activities such as working, playing, eating, reading, watching TV, etc. Create ate a graph to illustrate how you spend your time.

Books To Share:

Cosgrove, Stephen. *Leo The Lop (Tail Three)*
Spiers, Peter. *Bored - Nothing To Do*
Tusa, Tricia. *Stay Away From The Junkyard!*
Ziefert, Harriet. *When The TV Broke*

Winning Attitude

Objective

To encourage children to develop positive messages when feeling anxious.

Script

Positive thoughts help me when I am nervous.

Sit comfortably with your feet on the floor and your eyes closed. Take three long, deep breaths. (pause) Feel yourself relaxing more and more with each breath. Let the rhythm of the music calm you. Feel your muscles relax and your heart and breathing slow. Say to yourself, "I am calm and relaxed."

You are on a bus filled with people your own age. All the boys and girls are wearing baseball caps. Feel your seat gently rock back and forth. It seems that almost everyone is wearing a different colored baseball jersey. Red, green, orange, purple, blue, almost every color you can think of. You are proudly wearing the color of your baseball team. You are going to represent your team at the All Star Game, a contest of all the best players in your area.

As the bus continues toward the stadium, take a deep breath and exhale. Breathe in deeply again. As you exhale you notice feeling less nervous about the big game. Breathe in and out again. You feel calm, relaxed and proud to be an All Star. Your breathing is slow and relaxed. Look out of the bus window and see the stadium in the distance. As you get closer you begin to realize how large the ballpark really is. It has a huge scoreboard that shoots off fireworks when someone hits a homerun. Imagine yourself running around the bases with a rainbow of fireworks lighting up the air around you.(pause)

The bus stops. Grab your dufflebag and walk on to the field. The seats all around the park are quickly filling up with people. Take a deep breath and smell the freshly popped popcorn which will soon disappear into hundreds of hungry mouths. The field is like a bright green carpet. The weather is perfect. It's a great day for a ball game. The voice from the loudspeaker echoes throughout the stadium. The All Star game is about to begin.

You begin to get nervous. Your stomach is tight and your breathing is shallow. "Oh say can you see . . . " The crowd begins singing the National Anthem. Say to yourself three times, **"Positive thoughts help me when I am nervous. . . . "** (pause)

Take your position on the field. Breathe slowly in and out, in and out. Picture yourself playing well. It's the last inning. Your team is just barely ahead. Watch as the batter hits the ball toward you. It's almost like slow motion as it lifts higher into the air. Run back to the wall, never taking your eyes off the ball. Say to yourself "I know I can catch it". Jump as high as you can and make the best catch of your life. You have used positive self-talk to become the best player you can be.

Take a deep breath and return to your room. Open your eyes and stretch. (pause) Take a few moments to appreciate the good feelings that come with relaxation.

Discussion

What usually happens when a person tells him or herself that he or she cannot do something? Why does positive self-talk work? Give some examples when it has helped you. Do you have to be the best to be a winner?

Activity

• Use pressurized dots or labels from an office supply store to make stickers. Draw a design and write positive statements on them to use when you'd like to give yourself a positive message. Or use this recipe to make your own personal stickers.

Sticker Adhesive - 2 envelopes unflavored gelatin, 1 cup water, 1/2 tsp. peppermint extract (optional). Mix all ingredients in a small saucepan. Heat mixture over medium heat until gelatin is dissolved, stirring occasionally. Allow this "adhesive" to cool. Thoroughly coat the back of the child's art work by painting on the cooled adhesive. Allow to dry for two hours. Store the dried stickers between sheets of waxed paper. When ready to use, lick the sticker and attach to any paper surface.

Paint A Picture

Objective

To help children develop an appreciation of their contribution to the beautiful things around them and their responsibility to make the right decisions to maintain their ability to appreciate these things.

Script

I make the right decisions, because I care about myself.

Sit comfortably with your feet on the floor and your eyes closed. Take three long, deep breaths. (pause) Feel yourself relaxing more and more with each breath. Let the rhythm of the music calm you. Feel your muscles relax and your heart and breathing slow. Say to yourself, "I am calm and relaxed."

Picture yourself in a bright white room. The floor is white. The walls are white. The ceiling is white. It is perfectly quiet. You feel relaxed and calm. Look and see five large white jars. Walk over to the jars. Twist off the first cap and discover a thick rich green paint. Just like plants, this green gives off fresh oxygen. Breathe in and smell the green. Find a magic brush and begin to paint. Reach down and paint grass, plants and bushes. Reach up and paint large healthy trees. Hear the sounds of birds. Step back and enjoy your green scene.

Open the next jar and discover the bright beautiful red paint. Breathe in and smell the fragrance of your favorite flower. Take your magic brush and begin to paint red flowers on the white walls. Your brush allows you to make each flower look and smell real. With the tip of your brush paint a ladybug. Step back and enjoy your wonderful red world.

Twist off the next jar cover and find blue. Reach above your head. Stretch as high as you can and paint the ceiling. Move your arms back and forth until the entire sky is a beautiful blue. Hear the sound of an airplane flying. Step back and feel proud of your sky painting. Open the next jar to find yellow. This color reminds you of sunshine. Dip in your magic brush and reach for the sky. Extend your arms as much as possible and paint a big yellow sun. Your room becomes warmer and even more beautiful. Step back and enjoy the scene you have created. Dip your brush in the last jar. This clear paint allows you to add to your picture any color of the rainbow. Take a minute to paint in your favorite things about nature. (pause) There is beauty all around you. The more you look the more you see.

Take your magic paint brush and on a sign write the word NO in big letters. Put this large sign on one of the trees you have painted. This will always remind you to say NO! to anything that would keep you from appreciating the wonderful things around you. Breathe in deeply and repeat to yourself three times, **"I make the right decisions, because I care about myself . . . "** (pause) Remember to say NO! to alcohol, drugs and anything else that may keep you from being part of the positive and beautiful things around you.

Take a deep breath and return to your room. Open your eyes and stretch. (pause) Take a few moments to appreciate the good feelings that come with relaxation.

Discussion

Why is it important to care about yourself? Give an example of a good decision you made recently. Why is it sometimes hard to say no?

Activities

• Role play a scene where you say "NO!" to something that might hurt you, state the reason why you are saying no and state where you will go or what you will do instead. (Three elements: say no - state why - alternate action)
• What would your ideal day be like? Describe the events from the moment you wake up until the time you go to sleep that night.

Book To Share

Muller, Robin. *The Magic Paintbrush*

Time Travel

Objective

To help children create a visual image of feeling positive about getting older.

Script

I feel positive about my future.

Sit comfortably with your feet on the floor and your eyes closed. Take three long, deep breaths. (pause) Feel yourself relaxing more and more with each breath. Let the rhythm of the music calm you. Feel your muscles relax and your heart and breathing slow. Say to yourself, "I am calm and relaxed."

Imagine you are in the cockpit of an airplane. Fasten your seatbelt. Lean back on the soft large seat. Look at the many complicated dials and buttons in front of and above you. One large lever has a sign on it that says "time travel". Is it possible? In Ready . . . Set . . . R.E.L.A.X., almost anything is possible. Breathe slowly and reach out and grab the lever. Pull it toward you. Hear the engine start up. It purrs like a kitten. Feel the seat rock gently from side to side. See the most beautiful sights, as you begin to follow a rainbow into the future.

You have landed. Take a breath and relax. It is now next year. You feel warm and safe. Where are you? Look around, listen, hear, smell. How are you different? (pause) Think of how you would like to be in one year. You enjoy being a year older.

Reach out and pull the lever forward again. Follow the rainbow into the future. Take a deep breath and relax. The year is 20__, five years from now. You feel warm and safe. Where are you? Look around, listen, hear, smell. How will you be different five years from now? (pause)

You enjoy being five years older. Reach out and pull the lever for the third time. You again follow a rainbow to the future. This time you may land whenever you want as an adult. Take a deep breath and relax. You feel warm and safe. Where are you? Look around, listen, hear, smell. How will you be different as an adult? (pause) You enjoy being an adult. The future is fun to dream about, but you simply must get back to the present. Slowly push the lever back to it's original position. Hear your engine purr and feel your seat gently rock.

Take a refreshing breath, feeling calm and relaxed. As you travel back repeat the following phrase to yourself three times, **"I feel positive about my future . . . "** (pause) Your REAL trip into the future promises to be positive and exciting and it starts today.

Take a deep breath and return to your room. Open your eyes

Take a deep breath and return to your room. Open your eyes and stretch. (pause) Take a few moments to appreciate the good feelings that come with relaxation.

Discussion

What were some of your images about the future? What are some ways to plan for your future? What does it mean when you say "Today is the first day of the rest of your life?"

Activities

• Make a time capsule out of a shoebox or Pringles can. Draw pictures or write about things that are important to you today.

• Listen to the song "When You Wish Upon a Star" from the movie *Pinnocio*. Close your eyes and dream a dream about your future.

• Create a picture of outer space entitled, "The Sky's the Limit." Label each star with a goal you wish to achieve in the next five years, fifty years or your lifetime.

Books To Share

Kraus, Robert. *Leo The Late Bloomer*
Dr. Seuss. *Oh the Places You'll Go*

Music

"When you Wish Upon a Star" (*Pinochio*)
"The Rainbow Connection" (*The Muppet Movie*)
"Over the Rainbow" (*The Wizard of Oz*)

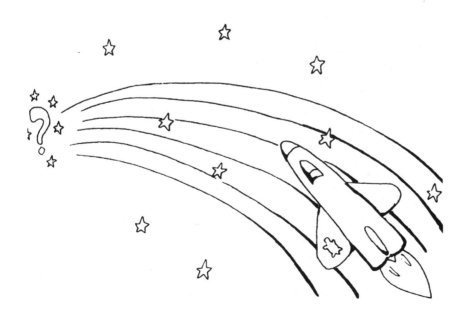

Dream On

Objective

To encourage students to take time to focus on the positive aspects of each day. To go to sleep with positive thoughts.

Script

I dream happy dreams.

Sit comfortably with your feet on the floor and your eyes closed. Take three long, deep breaths. (pause) Feel yourself relaxing more and more with each breath. Let the rhythm of the music calm you. Feel your muscles relax and your heart and breathing slow. Say to yourself, "I am calm and relaxed."

Breathe slowly. The light is dim. You are lying on a soft bed. The mattress gently hugs your entire body. Feel your toes, feet, legs, seat, back, arms and hands relax as they sink into the mattress. Your head rests on a large fluffy feather pillow. Feel the tension leave your shoulders, neck and head. Feel the tension leave your shoulders, neck and head as they sink into the pillow. Reach down and pull the sheet over your legs, stomach and up to your shoulders. Feel its cool softness relax the front of your body. Take a deep breath and smell the freshly washed sheet. It reminds you of a spring breeze. With the soft mattress on the bottom and the light sheet on top, you become a sandwich of relaxation. You are calm and relaxed. Listen to the music. (pause)

Look up at the ceiling fan above your bed. The glow of the moonlight in your room creates soft swirling shadows that dance across the ceiling. Concentrate on the fan. See the blades go round and round. (pause) The fans soft humming noise further relaxes you. As you watch the blades spin, see a picture of something good that happened to you today. Enjoy this scene. (pause) Take a deep breath, blink, and see a picture of something nice you did for someone else. Enjoy this scene. (pause) These pictures stay in your mind as your eyes become heavy and begin to close. You are comfortable and at peace. Reach over and grab a small toy or object next to your bed. Put it under your pillow. This is your "worry wart". It is handy because it will blow away all of your bad dreams for you. (pause) As your eyes close for the night, repeat to yourself three times, **"I dream happy dreams ... "** (pause) Promise yourself that tonight right before you go to sleep you will look up at your ceiling and see good things that happened today. Pleasant dreams!

Take a deep breath and return to your room. Open your eyes and stretch. (pause) Take a few moments to appreciate the good feelings that come with relaxation.

Discussion

Do you ever have trouble getting to sleep at night because something is bothering you? What could you use as a "worry wart" to put under your pillow?

Activity

• Smile Power Day. Write ten things that make you feel good about yourself.

Books to Share

Hoben, R. *Bedtime For Frances*
Meyer, M. *There's a Nightmare in My Closet*

Part III

Appendix
and
References

Appendix A

Introductory Letter to Parents
(using program on a school-wide basis)

Dear Parents:

This letter is to inform you of our plans to continue our effort to help children deal with stress in their lives. Mr. Jeff Allen, Principal, the teaching staff, and Dr. Roger Klein, school psychologist, have been developing this concept over the last year and are ready for full implementation during the upcoming school year.

The program is entitled Ready...Set...R.E.L.A.X. (Relax, Enjoy, Learn, Appreciate, Expand) and grew out of a concern for the need to help children learn to relax and tap into positive thinking.

The R.E.L.A.X. program will begin with an inservice for the children during the third week of school. During this meeting factual information about stress and a discussion about its psychological and physical effects will be presented by Mr. Allen and Dr. Klein. The children will then be led through a relaxation exercise intended to help them release tension from all the major muscle groups.

The R.E.L.A.X. program consists of scripts read over the intercom by Mr. Allen. These scripts along with soft music, are intended to help the children relax and think in a positive way. Examples are statements such as: I am filled with creative energy; I feel love and joy in my life; I enjoy using my imagination; I am positive minded; I enjoy learning new things; I learn about people before I judge them; Exercise makes me feel better; I tell someone I trust when I hurt inside.

The students will initially hear formal R.E.L.A.X. scripts three days per week immediately after lunch recess. On the other two days students will engage in quiet reading and listen to soft music.

As part of the program, the children will be asked to rate themselves on several inventories measuring perception of anxiety, depression and self concept. The students will be asked not to put their names on these as they are being used only to measure overall feelings before the program and at the end of the year.

A parent inservice will be held in the fall to answer any questions and to give a more detailed explanation of the R.E.L.A.X. program. If you have questions prior to that date, please call Mr. Allen.

We are excited about this positive attempt to equip our children with a concrete way to deal with stress in their lives and encourage you to begin using the R.E.L.A.X. concepts within your home.

We look forward to seeing you at the parent inservice.

Sincerely,

Jeff Allen, Principal

Roger Klein, School Psychologist

Appendix B

Ideas for Teacher Inservice

I. Psychophysiology of Stress—Stress Alarm Reaction Demon-
    stration
    A. All living things have an innate stress-alarm reaction. In
        humans the following occurs: *Adrenaline* and *nor-adrena-*
        line are released which increases heart rate, constricts blood
        vessels near outside of body, tenses muscles, increases res-
        piration rate, sharpens senses (pupils enlarge), increases
        perspiration, and aids in clotting blood. *Cortisone* is also
        released which raises blood pressure, produces glucose,
        and shuts down digestion.
    B. Negative vs. Positive Stress Response
        1. Positive—normal adaptive reaction, the source of
            stresses identifiable, challenge is met, individual re-
            turns to normal functioning.
        2. Negative—if stress is ambiguous, undefined, or pro-
            longed—or when several sources exist simulta-
            neously—the individual doesn't return to normal
            baseline as rapidly and continues to manifest a poten-
            tially damaging stress reaction.
    C. Demonstration of stress reaction (loud noise) or recall in-
        cident in which life was in danger—e.g. car accident, bad
        fall, etc.

II. Stress related psychological and physiological disorders #1
    social and health problem in last 20 years.
    A. Physical disorders where stress may play a factor:
        1. Cardiovascular disorders
        2. Cancer
        3. Arthritis
        4. Respiratory Disease
    B. 50-80% of all diseases are believed to be influenced by
        stress (e.g.'s ulcer, colitis, asthma, dermatitis, allergies,
        Raynaud's disease, hypertension, migraine, impotence, in-
        somnia, alcoholism, neurotic and psychotic disorders)

III. Need to reduce stress by understanding the power of thought
     and imagery. Our body responds to what our mind is think-
     ing
    A. Demonstrations
        1. Key on string—hold string between thumb and pointer
            finger with key tied to other end, arm extended 90

degree angle at elbow; think of key moving in a circle to right, left, stopping.
2. Demonstrate arm resistance: Put arms straight out, palms up, partner tries to push down; first with nothing said, then with negative comment, then with positive comment.

IV. Application to Athletics
   A. Athletes report that during competition their mental attitudes account for 80% or more of their success. Thoughts and feelings affect athletic performance. Application: need to give selves positive messages; (e.g.'s) blocking, free throws.
   B. Research findings
      1. Free throw shooting accuracy increases with use of visual imagery.
      2. Ability to detach and disassociate from external and internal stimuli while focusing on the task—U.S. Rhythmic Gymnastics team using GSR.
      3. Olympic Hockey Team beating Russians.
      4. Each thought has a corresponding neuromuscular movement.

V. Athletic Stress Groups
   A. Athletes are self-identified or recommended by coaches; meet once a week for ten weeks during a different period each week. Sessions include direct instruction about stress, sharing of concerns, practice in relaxation and success imagery. Advanced group also works on bio-feedback during the week.
   B. Each student develops a written script on self-improvement target, and records it with baroque or relaxing music in background.
   C. Each student develops ability to deeply relax and use guided imagery.
   D. Demonstrate Relaxation Response and Biofeedback.

VI. Results: N=50. The average score of 11 on the Beck Depression Scale pre-test fell to 5. The average %ile score on the Self Concept Scale increased from the pre-test score of 52 to a post-test score of 65. The %ile score on the anxiety scale fell from the pre-test score of 71 to the post-test score of 55.

VII. Application to the Classroom
   A. Research indicates that degree of stress is related to the degree of behavioral, learning and emotional problems among school age children. This places children who are under stress at risk.
   B. National Health Survey done in 1971 on cross-sectional

sample of 7,119 children age 6-11. The number of children who were rated by their parents as moderately tense or high strung increased from 40.7% to 48% by age eleven. Over 50% showed occasional or frequent strong temper.

C. Research shows positive results among children who have been exposed to a stress management program (e.g.)-
   1. Significant increase in achievement scores in fifth grade children in Clearwater, Florida Schools.
   2. Systematic desensitization has been successful in treatment of children's fears—has improved performance on tests when used with test anxiety students.
   3. Significant changes in attentiveness.
   4. Overall anxiety levels lowered.
   5. Lowered activity levels in hyperactive children.

VIII. Recommendations
   A. We are what we think—examine yourself physically, emotionally, spiritually.
   B. Be sensitive to your needs as well as your students'—both of you need positive strokes.
   C. Take one thing at a time.
   D. Learn to take things less seriously.
   E. Do things for others.
   F. Talk things over with others.

IX. In the end we can't eliminate stress but you can equip yourself and your students with the understanding of what stress is and the tools to deal with it. You, as teachers, are in a strategic position to influence many others and possibly make a life-long impact on helping children make healthy adjustments to stress.

X. Explanation of Ready . . . Set . . . R.E.L.A.X. Program.
   A. Research findings regarding use of muscle relaxation, music, active imagination.
   B. Instructions on administering inventories.
   C. Daily schedule.
   D. Questions and demonstration of relaxation through R.S.R. script.

Appendix C

Ideas for Student Presentation

I. What happens inside your body when you get nervous, anxious or scared?
   A. Explain the "fight or flight" response.
   B. Give examples of things that might cause this reaction:
      1. arguments.
      2. a scary movie.
      3. an accident.
   C. Ask for other examples.
   D. Point out the negative effects of prolonged stress.

II. Establish why it is important to learn how to relax.
   A. Counteracts stress.
   B. Improves concentration.
   C. Helps us get well when feeling sick
   D. Ask for other examples.

III. Discuss the power of the mind.
   A. Explain results of basketball experiment.
   B. Demonstrate key on string exercise.
   C. Demonstrate loss of muscle power with negative message.
   D. Define active imagination.

IV. Explain the importance of relaxing music.
   A. Explain experiment with plants.
   B. Play music.

V. Explain the Ready . . . Set . . . R.E.L.A.X. program.

VI. Lead the group in a muscle relaxation exercise and read a sample R.S.R. script.

Appendix D

Ideas for Parent Inservice

I.   Introduction.
  A. Self.
  B. Stress—Pressure from the outside that can make us feel tense inside.
    1. Some is important but too much can make us sick.
    2. Bodily reactions-pupils enlarge, blood vessels in bodily periphery constrict (in case of a wound), heart speeds up, stomach and intestines shut down, adrenaline pumped into blood, respiration increases.
    3. Prolonged stress leads to hormonal imbalance and deterioration of the immune system.
  C. How stress affects children has not been a focus of attention in the past. Research has been done only relatively recently.
  D. Parent input—what have you observed in regard to stress? First in your own childhood and next in your children or other children of today, e.g.—change in families, abuse, AODA concerns, media, etc.

II. Some Research Findings.
  A. Martha Vineyard Child Health Survey; Longitudinal began in 1976; 400 children, age 12 months to 6 years; looked at the kinds of stress that are most damaging to children. Findings:
    1. Chronic stress producing difficulties in families in rank order:
      a. Financial security.
      b. Housing.
      c. Work.
      d. Marriage conflict.
      e. Health problems.
    2. Kinds of stress most damaging to children:
      a. Marital discord and psychiatric problems on part of parent (e.g. depression) were strongly associated with behavioral difficulties in young children.
      b. Chronic continual stress much more damaging than isolated cases.
      c. Boys are more vulnerable than girls.
  B. Children generally convert stress into behavioral disorders:
    1. Over activity.

    2. Sleep problems.
    3. Bed wetting.
    4. Eating problems.
    5. Fears.
    6. Poor social relationships.
C. Average number of stressful events experienced by families during the year was 6.2.
D. One of the main causes of stress is change—e.g. loss, illness, change in lifestyle, job changes, money problems, family change.
    1. Change creates tension which in turn creates anxiety or a worried uptight feeling or vague fear that something bad or unpleasant is going to happen.
    2. Continuous anxiety leads to depression.

III. To children stress is comprised of what they worry about; what scares them; what they get excited about; what they think about. Age group breakdowns according to Dean Coddington from the L.S.U. medical school are the following:
A. Elementary Children.
    1. Squabbles with parents.
    2. Reprimands.
    3. Physical fights with peers.
    4. Being alone.
B. Middle School.
    1. Arguments with parents and friends.
    2. Tests.
    3. Violent weather, threat of nuclear war.
    4. Puberty (explain cognitive changes).
C. Senior High.
    1. Non-acceptance.
    2. Dating.
    3. Looks.
    4. Drugs and alcohol.
    5. Sexual discussions.

IV. David Elkind—(*The Hurried Child: Growing Up Too Fast Too Soon*)
A. Feels children are being hurried through childhood. On the outside they look and act very mature but on the inside they are still children.
B. He feels we socially expect too much of them—force them to make decisions and deal with situations that demand maturity they don't have.
C. Academically encourage vs. pressure—parents often bribe children to learn to read earlier and achieve faster.
    1. Kids learn that to be acceptable they must produce a product. Its easy to fall into that trap because the school

system is set up that way. Birth to six years children ask the questions. But what happens when they get into school? The school now asks the questions and if the kids don't have the right answers. . . . (lead discussion)

2. It is not healthy for children to have to earn adults' attention and love by producing more and more. Give examples. Ask for examples.

V. Recommendations.
   A. View parenting as a vocation.
   B. Examine yourself. . .
      1. Physically—Taking care of yourself is the best
      2. Emotionally—Things you can do for your children.
      3. Spiritually.
   C. Minimize stress in child's life.
      1. Realistic expectations.
      2. Allow yourself and them to be average in some things.
      3. Examine environment—e.g.. noise, music, reading material, videos.
   D. Be sensitive to your own and your child's needs.
      1. Even though a child's worries may seem trivial to us they are extremely significant to him/her. (e.g.) Erma Bombeck's book *Motherhood: The Second Oldest Profession*, describes a child's fears on the first day of school: "What if my loose tooth wants to come out when we're supposed to have our heads down and be quiet?"
      "What if I splash water on my name tag and my name disappears and no one will know who I am?"
      A nursery school child "What if I sneeze—I can't go to school!" (one child was sneezing just prior to moving out of town)
   E. Be observant of changes in your own and your child's behavior.
      1. Eating, sleeping, temperament, academic performance, reaction to sitters.
      2. Trust your intuition—listen to your child.
   F. Recognize value of play in your own and your child's life.
      1. Play is the way children work through stress—should not be competitive or pressured—encourage creativity, paper, crayons, paint, clay.
      2. Take walks with child, play with them.
      3. Reassure them you love them, cuddle, hug, kiss.
      4. Encourage recreational activities for enjoyment.
      5. Turn off the T.V.
   G. Teach your children the power of faith and a positive outlook.
      1. Our thoughts influence our emotions, strength, self-concept, etc.

2. Teach by your example—be positive—practice your faith.
3. Help yourself and your child to use a visual tool to alleviate stress—(e.g.) flash a "STOP" sign and substitute a positive thought.
4. Write or draw fears—especially good with nightmares.

H. Establish your priorities—parenting has to be #1.
   1. Help child make decisions and choose priorities.
      a. (e.g.) too many choices—help them think through choices and consider consequences.
      b. dividing big responsibilities into smaller chunks . . . must learn this . . . doesn't come naturally.
   2. Help child organize plans for the day.

I. Teach child good health habits and show by your example.
   1. Physical-relaxing, breathing slowing, massages, rocking.
   2. Emotional—use bedtime to establish a routine, talking, reading, reassuring, tucking in, talking about feelings, guided fantasy .
   3. Improve your knowledge about stress.

VI. Conclusion: In the end we can't eliminate stress but we can equip our children with the understanding of what stress is and the tools to deal with it. We can also help by giving the extra individual attention, love and understanding that children need. Build memories with your children. Be there now so they learn how to deal with life and take an active part in it and not be crippled by stress.

VII. Explanation of Ready . . . Set . . . R.E.L.A.X. Program.
   A. Research on active imagination, muscle relaxation, music & demonstration of R.S.R.

Appendix E

Student Questionnaire/Evaluation

_____   _____
(Name is optional.)   Grade

Please answer the following questions about the R.S.R. Program. Your reactions and ideas will be very helpful in planning for next year. Thank you.

1. Do you actively participate in R.S.R.? ____Yes ____No

2. Is having R.S.R. after the noon recess the best time?
    ____Yes ____No

    If no, when would be a better time?

3. How do you usually feel before R.S.R. time?

4. How do you usually feel after participating in R.S.R.?

5. Can you name the theme of your favorite R.S.R. script of this year?

    The one about_____

6. What do you think about the music played during R.S.R. time?

7. Have you ever used R.S.R. outside the classroom?
    ___Yes ___No

    If yes, please say when and where:

8. What things would make the R.S.R. Program more useful to students?

9. Do you have any ideas for R.S.R. stories? Places we can visit?

    Things we can do?

10. Do you want us to continue the R.S.R. program next year?
    ___Yes ___No

    If no, why not?

Ready . . . Set . . . R.E.L.A.X.
Student Journal

A journal is a written record of your stories, ideas, dreams or daydreams.
Very often, journals are written every day.
If a thought or idea comes to mind after
a *Ready . . . Set . . . R.E.L.A.X.* activity,
you may write it below.

1. _____   2. _____
_____   _____
_____   _____
_____   _____
_____   _____
_____   _____

3. _____   4. _____
_____   _____
_____   _____
_____   _____
_____   _____
_____   _____

5. _____   6. _____
_____   _____
_____   _____
_____   _____
_____   _____
_____   _____

Ready . . . . Set . . . . R.E.L.A.X.

Certificate of Completion

READY SET RELAX ★ READY SET RELAX ★

R.S.R.

READY SET RELAX ★ READY SET RELAX ★

Has participated in a program to encourage learning and positive self-esteem through the use of relaxation and imagination.

Signature

Date

About the Authors

ROGER KLEIN has worked with children and parents since entering the field of education in 1971. His background includes classroom teaching, coaching and school psychology. He is currently working part time as a school psychologist in Watertown, Wisconsin and the remaining time as a private practice clinical psychologist.

Roger has presented the concepts of using music, relaxation and active imagination at the national, state and local levels. He has a masters of arts degree in counseling and an educational specialists degree in school psychology from the University of Northern Colorado. He completed his doctorate degree in clinical psychology, with special emphasis in children and adolescents, at the Wisconsin School of Professional Psychology.

JEFFREY ALLEN has been a special education, elementary education teacher and school administrator in Wisconsin since 1975. He is presently the principal of a pre-K to 6 elementary school.

Jeffrey has both an undergraduate and graduate degree in education from the University of Wisconsin-Whitewater. He has written and directed numerous plays, musicals and video productions for children. He has also contributed articles and photographs in local and national professional publications. For the past ten years he has organized and facilitated support groups for families experiencing death, divorce or separation. In addition, Allen serves as a coordinator for Odyessey of the Mind, the "Olympics" of creativity for children.

References

Adler, R. (1983). Developmental psychoneuroimmunology. *Developmental Psychobiology, 16,* 251–267.

Battle, J. (1987). *Depression inventory for children and adults.* San Francisco: Northern California Medical Services, Inc. in affiliation with Children's Hospital of San Francisco Publication Department.

Bellanger, R. G. (1981). The effects of relaxation training on self-concept. *Dissertation Abstracts International, 41,* 2936A.

Belsky, J. (1980). Child maltreatment: An ecological integration. *American Psychologist, 35.* 320–335.

Benson, H. (1976). *The relaxation response.* New York: Avon Books.

Bernstein, D. A., & Borkovec, T. D. (1973). *Progressive relaxation training: A manual for the helping professionals.* Champaign, Ill.: Research Press.

Bieliauskas, L. A. (1982). *Stress and its relationship to health and illness.* New York: Westview Press.

Brenner, A. (1984). *Helping children cope with stress.* Lexington, Mass.: Lexington Books.

Bronfenbrenner, V. (1979). *The ecology of human development.* Cambridge: Harvard University Press.

Brown, J. M., O'Keefe, J. O., Sanders, S. H., & Baker, B. (1986). Developmental changes in children's cognition to stressful and painful situations. *Journal of Pediatric Psychology, 11* (3), 343–357.

Brown, R. H. (1977). An evaluation of the effectiveness of relaxation as a treatment modality for the hyperactive child. *Dissertation Abstracts International, 38* (6B), 2847.

Cannon, W. B. (1914). The emergency function of the adrenal medulla in pain and major emotions. *American Journal of Physiology, 33,* 356–372.

Carter, J. L., & Russell, H. L. (1985). Use of EMG biofeedback procedures with learning disabled children in a clinical and an educational setting. *Journal of Learning Disabilities, 18,* 213–216.

Carter, J. L., Russell, H. L. (1982). EEG Alpha and Beta Training for learning disabled boys with intellectual verbal-performance IQ discrepancies. In J. H. Humphrey (Ed.), *Stress in Childhood.* New York: AMS Press, Inc.

Cauce, A. M., Comer, J. P., & Schwartz, D. (1987). Long term effects of a systems-oriented school prevention program. *American Journal of Orthopsychiatry, 57* (1), 127–131.

Chang, J., & Hiebert, B. (1989). Relaxation procedures with children: A review. *Medical Psychotherapy, 2,* 163–176.

Cobb, D. E., & Evans, J.R. (1981). The use of biofeedback techniques with school-aged children exhibiting behavioral and/or learning problems. *Journal of Abnormal Child Psychology, 9,* 251–281.

Cratty, B. J. (1972). *Physical expressions of intelligence*. Englewood Cliffs: Prentice-Hall Inc., 144–145.

D'Alelio, W. A., & Murray, E. J. (1981). Cognitive therapy for test anxiety. *Cognitive Therapy and Research, 5*, 299–307.

Day, R. C. & Sadek, S. N. (1982). The effect of Benson's relaxation response on the anxiety levels of Lebanese children under stress. *Journal of Experimental Child Psychology, 34*, 350–356.

Deffenbacher, J. L., & Kemper, C. C. (1977). Counseling test-anxious sixth graders. *Elementary School Guidance and Counseling, 9*, 22–29.

Deffenbacher, J. L., Michaels, A. C., Daley, P. C., & Michaels, T. (1980). A comparison of homogeneous and heterogeneous anxiety management training. *Journal of Counseling Psychology, 27*, 630–634.

Dendato, K. M., & Drener, D. (1986). Effectiveness of cognitive/relaxation therapy and study-skills training in reducing self-reported anxiety and improving the academic performance of test-anxious students. *Counseling Psychology, 33* (2), 131–135.

Disorbio, J. M. (1983). The effects of the kiddie quieting response on stress and anxiety of elementary school children. *Dissertation Abstracts International, 44* (11), 3523–B.

Elkind, D. (1981). *The hurried child*. New York: Addison Wesley.

Engel, B. T., & Schneiderman, N. (1984). Operant conditioning and the modulation of cardiovascular function. *Annual Review of Physiology, 46*. 199–210.

Engel, B.T. (1972). *Handbook of Psychophysiology*. New York: Holt, Rinehart, and Winston.

Eron, L. D. (1982). Parent-child interaction, television violence, and aggression of children. *American Psychologist, 37* (2), 197–211.

Finch, A. J., & Rogers, R. T. (1984). Self-report instruments. In T. Ollendick & M. Hersen (Eds.), *Child behavioral assessment: Principles and procedures*. New York: Pergamon Press.

Fiske, E. B. (1986, April). Early schooling is now the rage. *New York Times*, pp. 24–30.

Flanders, P. & McNamara J. R. (1987). Relaxation training and home practice in the treatment of anxiety. *Psychological Reports, 61*, 819–22.

Foley, M. A. & Johnson, M. K. (1985). Confusions between memories for performed and imagined actions: A development comparison. *Child Development, 56*, 1145–1155.

Folkman, S. & Lazarus R. (1985). Methodological issues in stress research. In A. Eichler, D. Silverman, and H. Pratt (Eds.), *How to define and research stress*, (pp. 95–104). Washington D.C.: American Psychiatric Press, Inc.

Forman, S. (1985). A school-based approach to stress management education of students. *Special Services in the Schools, 1* (3), 61–71.

Forman, S., O'Malley, P. (1985). A school-based approach to stress management education of students. *Special Services in the Schools, 1*, 61–71.

Freedman, M.,& R. H. Rosenman. (1974). *Type A behavior and your heart*. New York: Alfred A. Knopf.

Garman, S. L. (1985). *The therapeutic use of mental imagery: A review of recent empirical literature*. (Doctoral dissertation, Rosemead School of Psychology, Biola University). (ERIC Document Reproduction Service No. ED 273892).

Gatewood, E. L. (1921). The psychology of music in relation to anesthesia. *American Journal of Surgery, Anesthesia Supplement, 35*, 47–50.

George, L. (1986). Mental imagery enhancement training in behavior therapy: Current status and future prospects. *Psychotherapy, 23*, 81–92.

Gerber, E. R., & Danilson, H. A. (1984). The quieting reflex and success imagery. *Elementary School Guidance and Counseling. 12*, 152–155.

Greeson, L. E. & Zigarmi, D. (1985). Piaget, learning theory, and mental imagery: toward a curriculum of visual thinking. *Journal of Humanistic Education and Development, 24*, 40–49.

Guyer, N. P., & Guyer, C. G. (1984). Implementing relaxation training in counseling emotionally healthy adolescents: A comparison of three modes. *American Mental Health Counselors Association Journal, 6*, 79–87.

Hawkes, T. H., & Furst, N. F. (1971). Research notes: Race, socioeconomic situation, achievement, IQ, and teacher ratings of students' behavior as factors relating to anxiety in upper elementary children. *Sociology of Education, 44*, 333–350.

Hershey, M. (1983). Warm fingers, cool behavior. *Academic Therapy, 18*, 593–597.

Herzog, S. (1982). *Joy in the classroom*. Boulder Creek, CA: University Press.

Hiebert, B., & Eby, W. (1985). The effects of relaxation training on the school performance of Grade 12 students. *School Counselor, 32*, 205–210.

Hill, K. T. & Sarason, S. B. (1966). The relationship of test anxiety and defensiveness to test and school performance over the elementary years; a farther longitudinal study. *Monograph of the Society for Research in Child Development, 31* (2, Serial No. 104).

Hill, K. T. (1963). The relationship of test anxiety, defensiveness, and intelligence to sociometric status. *Child Development, 34*, 767–776.

Holland, M., Stroebel, C. & Stroebel, E. (1980) *Instructor's manual for QR for young people*. Wethersfield, CT: QR Institute.

Horan, J. J. (1980). Experimentation in counseling and psychotherapy part I: New myths about old realities. *Educational Researcher, 9*, 5–10.

Hume, D. 1748. *An inquiry concerning human understanding*. Chicago: Open Court, Reprinted 1907, 252–254.

Humphrey, J. H. & Humphrey, J. N. (1980). *How teachers can cope with stress*. College Park, Md.: AMS Press, Inc., 48.

Humphrey, J. H. & Humphrey, J. N. (1983). *Reducing stress in chil-*

dren through creative relaxation. Springfield, Ill.: Charles Thomas Publisher, 64.

Humphrey, J. H. & Humphrey, J. N. (Eds.) (1984). *Stress in childhood.* New York: AMS Press, Inc.

Humphrey, J. H. (1988). *Children and stress.* New York: AMS Press, Inc., 46.

Hunter, S. & Wolf, T. (1981). Type A coronary-prone behavior pattern and cardiovascular risk factor variables in children and adolescents. *Journal of Chronic Disease, 35,* 613–621.

Hunter, S., & Berenson, A. D., (1983). *Type A coronary-prone behavior pattern and cardiovascular risk factor variables in children and adolescents.* New York: Pergoman Press, Inc.

Jacobson, E. (1944). *Progressive relaxation.* Chicago: University of Chicago Press.

Johnson, B. M. (1979). The use of electromyography and relaxation in the reduction of tension in families with identified hyperactive children (Doctoral dissertation, United States International University, 1977). *Dissertation Abstracts International, 39,* 5560B.

Johnson, D. I., & Spielberger, C. D. (1968). The effects of relaxation training and the passage of time on measures of static and trait anxiety. *Journal of Clinical Psychology, 2,* 222–239.

Kahn, S. B. (1969). Affective correlates of academic achievement. *Journal of Educational Psychology, 60,* 215–221.

Kelton, A. & Belar, C. D. (1983). The relative efficacy of autogenic phrases and autogenic-feedback training in teaching handwarming to children. *Biofeedback & Self-Regulation, 8,* 461–475.

Klein, R. J. (1990). The effects of sedative music, muscle relaxation and success imagery on self-report of anxiety, self-concept and depression among elementary school children (doctoral dissertation, Wisconsin School of Professional Psychology, 1990). *Dissertation Abstracts International.*

Klein, S. A., & Deffenbacher, J. L. (1977). Relaxation and exercise for hyperactive impulsive children. *Perceptual and Motor Skills, 45,* 1159–1162.

Lazarus, R. S. (1971). The concepts of stress and disease. In L. Levi (Ed.), *The psychosocial environment and psychosomatic disease* (pp. 53–58). London: Oxford University Press.

Lazarus, R., and Folkman, S. (1984). *Stress, appraisal, and coping.* New York: Springer.

Levine, M. & Perkins, D. V. (1980). Social setting intervention and primary prevention: comments on the report of the task panel on prevention to the President's Commission on Mental Health. *American Journal of Community Psychology. 8,* 147–157.

Lighthall, F. F. (1959). Change in mental ability as a function of test anxiety and type of mental test. *Journal of Consulting Psychology, 23,* 34–38.

Loffredo, D. A., Omizo, M., & Hammett, V. L. (1984). Group relaxation training and parental involvement with hyperactive boys. *Journal of Learning Disabilities, 17,* 210–213.

Logan, T. G., & Roberts, A. R. (1984). The effects of different types of relaxation music on tension level. *Journal of Music Therapy, 21,* 177–183.

Lozanor, G., & Balevsky, D. (1975). The effect of the suggestopedia system of instruction on the physical development, state of health, and working capacity of first and second grade pupils. *Suggestology and Suggestopedia, 1* (No. 3), 21.

Lundberg, V. (1983). Note on Type A behavior and cardiovascular responses to challenge in 3–6 year old children. *Journal of Psychosomatic Research, 27,* 39–42.

Lupen, M., Braud, L. W., Braud, W., & Derer, W. (1976). Children, parents, and relaxation tapes. *Academic Therapy, 12,* 105–113.

Mason, J. W. (1968). A review of psychoendocrine research on the pituitary-adrenal cortical system. *Psychosomatic Medicine. 30,* 576–607.

Mason, J. W. (1975). A historical view of the stress field. *Journal of Human Stress. 3,* 7–36.

Matthews, D. (1983, March). *Relaxation training: A stress management model for schools.* Paper presented at the Annual Convention of the American Personnel and Guidance Association. Washington, D.C.

Matthews, D. (1986 February). *Stress management model for the elementary/middle/high school.* Paper presented at the Annual Meeting of the Association of Teacher Educators. Atlanta, GA.

Matthews, K. (1982). Psychological perspectives on the Type A behavior pattern. *Psychological Bulletin, 91,* 293–323.

Matthews, K., & Angulo, J. (1980) Measurement of the Type A behavior pattern in children: Assessment of children's competitiveness, impatience-anger, and aggression. *Child Development, 51,* 466–475.

McManus, J. (1984, April). *Overview of stress effects on body and stress prevention techniques.* Paper presented at the Annual Convention of the National Association of School Psychologists. Philadelphia, PA.

McNamce, A. (1982). *Children and stress.* Washington, D.C., Association for Childhood Education International.

Mead, R. J. (1976). The effects of relaxation training on the attitudes and anxiety levels of 9th grade potential dropouts. *Dissertation Abstracts International, 37* (9A), 5612.

Meichenbaum, D. (1977). *Cognitive-behavior modification: An integrative approach.* New York: Plenum.

Middleton, W. W., Ray, P. W., Kerry, W. A., & Amft, R. (1944). The effect of music on feelings of restfulness-tiredness and pleasantness-unpleasantness. *Journal of Psychology, 17,* 299–318.

Miller, R. K. & Bornstein, P. H. (1977). Thirty-minute relaxation: A comparison of some methods. *Journal of Behavior Therapy and Experimental Psychiatry, 8,* 291–294.

O'Reilly, P., & Weghtman, L. E. (1971). Improving the identification of anxious elementary school children through the use of an adjusted anxiety scale. *Journal of Educational Measurement, 8,* 107–112.

Ostrander, S. & Schroeder, L. *Super learning.* (1979). New York: Dell Publishing Co., 84.

Padamer, D. D. (1977). Reading performance of relaxation trained children. *Dissertation Abstracts International, 37* (2B), 978.

Phillips, B. N., Martin, R. P., & Meyers, J. (1972). Interventions in relation to anxiety in school. In C.D. Spielberger (Ed.), *Anxiety: Current trends in theory and research (Vol. 2).* New York: Academic Press.

Piaget, J., & Inhelder, B. (1971). *Mental imagery in the child.* New York: Basic Books.

Piers, E. V. & Harris, D. B. Age and other correlates of self-concept in children. *Journal of Educational Psychology,* 1964, *55,* No. 2, 91–95.

Postman, N. (1981, January). T.V.'s disastrous impact on children. *U.S. News and World Report.* pp. 43–45.

Proeger, C. & Myrick, R.D. (1987). *Teaching children to relax.* Samble, Florida: Florida Educational Research and Development Council, Inc.

Retallack, D. (1973). *The sound of music and plants.* Marina del Rey: Devorss and Co.

Richter, N. C. (1984). The efficacy of relaxation training with children. *Journal of Abnormal Child Psychology, 12,* 319–344.

Rosenthal, M. K. (1977). The effect of a novel situation and anxiety on two groups of dependency behaviors. *British Journal of Psychology, 58,* 357–364.

Ross, D. M. & Ross, S. A. (1984). Childhood pain: the school-aged child's viewpoint. *Pain, 20,* 179–191.

Rozensky, R. H., & Pasternak, J. P. (1985). Obi-Wan Kenobi, "The Force," and the art of biofeedback: A headache treatment for overachieving young boys. *Clinical Biofeedback & Health, 8,* 9–13.

Ruebush, B. (1973). Child Psychology. In H. Stevenson, J. Kagan, and C. Spiher (Eds.), *The 62nd yearbook of the national society for the study of education (part 1).* Chicago: The University of Chicago Press.

Salholz, E. (1982, August 9). Beware of child molesters. *Newsweek,* pp. 45–57.

Sarason, I. G. (1972). Experimental approaches to test anxiety: attention and use of information. In C.D. Spielberger (Ed.), *Anxiety: Current trends in theory and research (Vol. 2).* New York, Academic Press.

Sarason, I. G. (1980). Introduction to the study of test anxiety. In I. G. Sarason (Ed.), *Test anxiety: Theory, research, and applications.* Hillsdale, N.J.: Erlbaum.

Sarason, S. B., Davidson, K. S., Lighthall, F. F., Waite, R. R., & Ruebush, B. K. (1960). *Anxiety in elementary school children: a report of research.* New York: Wiley.

Sarason, S. B., Hill, K. T. & Zimardo, P. G. (1964). A longitudinal study of the relation of test anxiety to performance on intelligence and achievement tests. *Monographs of the Society for Research in Child Development, 29,* (7, Serial No. 98).

Selye, H. (1936). A syndrome produced by diverse nocuous agents. *Nature, 138*, 32.

Selye, H. (1950). *The physiology and pathology of exposure to stress.* Montreal, Octa Inc.

Selye, H. (1956). *The stress of life.* New York: McGraw-Hill Book Co., Inc.

Sheikh, A. A. & Jordan, C. S. (1983). Clinical use of mental imagery. In A.A. Sheikh (Ed.), *Imagery: Current theory, research, and application* (pp. 391–435). New York: John Wiley and Sons.

Speidel, G. E. & Troy, M. E. (1985). The ebb and flow of mental imagery in education. In A.A. Sheikh and S. Sheikh (Eds.), *Imagery in Education*, (pp. 11–38). Farmingdale, N.Y.: Baywood Publishing.

Spillios, J. C., & Janzen, H. L. (1983). The effect of relaxation therapy on achievement for anxious learning disabled students. *School Psychology International, 4*, 101–107.

Suzuki, N. S. (1985). Imagery research with children: Implications for education. In A. A. Sheikh & K. S. Sheikh (Eds.), *Imagery in Education* (pp. 179–198). Farmingdale, New York: N.Y.: Baywood Publishing.

Tobias, S. (1980). Math anxiety: What you can do about it. *Today's Education, 69* (3), 26–29.

Turkkan, J.S., Brady, J.V., & Harris, A. H. (1982). Animal studies of stressful interactions: A behavioral physiological overview. In L. Goldberger and L. Brenitz (Eds.), *Handbook of Stress.* New York: Mac Millan.

Weigel, C., & Wertlieb, D. (1986). Social support as a moderator of children's stressful life experiences. *Psychosomatic Medicine, 48*, 3–4.

Wertlieb, D., Weigel, C., & Feldstein, M. (1987). Measuring children's coping. *American Journal of Orthopsychiatry. 57* (4), 548–560.

Wesecky, A. (1986). Music therapy for children with rett syndrom. *American Journal of Medical Genetics, 24*, 253–257.

Wesserman, A. L. (1988). Psychogenic basis for abdominal pain in children and adolescents. *Journal of the American Academy of Child and Adolescent Psychiatry, 27*, 179–84.

Whiting, H. T. A. (1969). *Acquiring ball skills.* Philadelphia: Lea and Febiger.

Williams, R. B. (1985). Neuroendocrine response patterns and stress: Biobehavioral mechanisms of disease. In R.B. Williams (Ed.), *Perspectives in Behavioral Medicine: Neuroendocrine Control and Behavior.* New York: Academic Press.

Wilson, N. H., & Rotter, J. C. (1986). Anxiety management training and study skills counseling for students on self-esteem and test anxiety and performance. *The School Counselor, 9*, 18–31.

Wolf, T., Sklov, M., Wenzl, P., Hunter, S., & Berenson, G. (1982). Validation of a measure of Type A behavior pattern in children: Begolusa heart study. *Child Development, 53*, 126–135.

Wolff, H.G. (1953). *Stress and Disease.* Springfield, Il.: Thomas.

Wolpe, J. (1958). *Psychotherapy by Reciprocal Inhibition*. Standford, California: Standford University Press.

Wright, J. (1978). An investigation of the effectiveness of a relaxation training model on discipline referrals. *Dissertation Abstracts International, 39* (4A), 2162.

Yuille, J. C. (1985). A laboratory-based experimental methodology is inappropriate for the study of mental imagery. *Journal of Mental Imagery, 9* (2), 137–150.

Zaichkowsky, L. B., & Zaichkowsky, L. D. (1984). The effects of a school-based relaxation training program on fourth grade children. *Journal of Clinical Child Psychology. 13*, 81–85.

Zill, N. (1977). *National survey of children's fears and aspirations*. Unpublished manuscript, Foundation for Child Development, 20.

Index